D0456110

1% Better

1% Better

REACHING MY FULL POTENTIAL
AND **HOW YOU CAN TOO**

Chris Nikic & Nik Nikic

WITH **DON YAEGER**

W Publishing Group

An Imprint of Thomas Nelson

© 2021 Chris Nikic and Nik Nikic

All rights reserved. No portion of this book may be reproduced, stored in
a retrieval system, or transmitted in any form or by any means—electronic,
mechanical, photocopy, recording, scanning, or other—except for brief
quotations in critical reviews or articles, without the prior written permission of
the publisher.

Published in Nashville, Tennessee, by W Publishing Group, an imprint of
Thomas Nelson.

Thomas Nelson titles may be purchased in bulk for educational, business,
fundraising, or sales promotional use. For information, please email
SpecialMarkets@ThomasNelson.com.

IRONMAN® and 70.3®, and their respective logos, are registered trademarks of
World Triathlon Corporation in the United States and other countries.

This independent publication has not been authorized, endorsed, sponsored
or licensed by, nor has content been reviewed or otherwise approved by, World
Triathlon Corporation, d/b/a The IRONMAN Group.

Any internet addresses, phone numbers, or company or product information
printed in this book are offered as a resource and are not intended in any way
to be or to imply an endorsement by Thomas Nelson, nor does Thomas Nelson
vouch for the existence, content, or services of these sites, phone numbers,
companies, or products beyond the life of this book.

The information in this book has been carefully researched, and all efforts
have been made to ensure accuracy. The author and the publisher assume no
responsibility for any injuries suffered or damages or losses incurred during or
as a result of following the exercise program in this book. All of the procedures,
poses, and postures should be carefully studied and clearly understood before
attempting them at home. Always consult your physician or qualified medical
professional before beginning this or any exercise program.

ISBN 978-0-7852-5645-8 (eBook)

Library of Congress Control Number: 2021940095

ISBN 978-0-7852-5618-2 (TP)

Printed in the United States of America

21 22 23 24 25 LSC 10 9 8 7 6 5 4 3 2 1

To my Grandpa Marko and Grandpa Jack
in heaven, I miss you both.

To my Grandma Luba and
Grandma Liz, I love you so much.

To my sister, Jacky, for always being there for me.
—CHRIS

I dedicate this book to my wife, my dream, the rock
of our family. Without you, none of this is possible.
Thank you for being the best wife and
mother. I love you forever.
—NIK

CONTENTS

Introduction: The Doctor's Office ix

PART 1

1 FROM MONTENEGRO TO THE BRONX 3
2 WORK AND FAMILY 17
3 CHRIS IS BORN 29
4 TOO WEAK TO NURSE 37
5 SCHOOL AND SPORTS 47

PART 2

6 NEW SETBACKS, NEW RESOLVE 57
7 LET'S DO ONE MORE 71
8 TEAM CHRIS 83
9 "YOU ARE AN IRONMAN!" 101

Contents

PART 3

10 GETTING TO 1% BETTER 117

11 LESSONS FOR ACHIEVING A
    1% BETTER MINDSET. 129

12 FUN, PAINLESS, AND HABIT-FORMING:
    The Good Life 143

13 THE ACHIEVEMENT-HABIT MINDSET 153

14 NOW IT'S YOUR TURN. 169

Acknowledgments 173

Appendix: The 1% Better System 179

Notes 197

About the Authors 199

INTRODUCTION
The Doctor's Office

Every journey—even the 2.4-mile swim, the 112-mile bike ride, and the 26.2-mile run of an IRONMAN® triathlon—has a starting line. This journey began in a nondescript doctor's office in suburban Maryland.

If you've ever had a child, you know it's a magical and sacred time. Nothing prepares you for the first time—the feelings of anticipation, excitement, and nervousness that come from knowing you're going to be responsible for the life of somebody other than yourself. Up until that moment, you've just been . . . you, which is to say somebody's son or daughter, then somebody's husband or wife. Getting married poses a big change in identity but is still not as transformative as becoming a parent.

My wife, Patty, and I had our first child in 1989, a beautiful baby girl named Jacky. Her birth weight was just shy of nine pounds, which meant she practically hit the ground running and hasn't slowed down since. So we had experienced this joyous anticipation before. Now it was ten years later, and after two miscarriages and serious concern that we might be unable to bring a brother or sister into the world for Jacky, Patty was once again pregnant. If you or a loved one have experienced a miscarriage, you know how devastating it can be, especially to the mother. Having a miscarriage can eat away at the mother's confidence and belief in her fitness for motherhood. As a father, even after all these years, I think of what could have been. I wonder what life would have been like with those two lost children. The thought never leaves me.

As a husband of a woman who has had a miscarriage, you can offer assurances to her that she is not alone in her time of doubting, but ultimately it is the mother's burden to bear. Despite having endured two miscarriages, Patty's and my dream finally came true, and we were just as excited about our second child as we were for the first. After all, a decade is a long time.

It was spring 1999, and Patty and I were sitting in the doctor's office in Westminster, Maryland, waiting for her ultrasound appointment. Patty had been through pregnancy before and was bolder than I was when it came to really digging in and asking doctors the hard questions, so she could have handled the visit on her own and shared all she learned with me that night. But I wanted to be there. We had spent ten long years trying to have a second child, and I wanted to be by her side. It was a good thing too.

Patty was in her second trimester, which is an especially exciting time because the embryo has begun to look like a real person with arms and legs and even little facial features. We both were excited when her turn came to see the doctor, and she went into the procedure room to be prepped by the technician. The procedure is typically carried out by a technician who uses a sonogram to record images of the child, which the doctor later evaluates before meeting with the expectant parents.

The tech moved the transducer around Patty's belly while she looked up at a monitor at all the weird images that flitted in and out of the screen until he got an image of the child. And there he was—that was going to be our son. Patty and I smiled and snuck a look over at the tech as he examined very closely images of the brain, heart, and spine. After a moment he made hard copies of the images and excused himself without saying much. Patty said she felt a little awkward, and a little bit of concern crept into her mind at the technician's whispers in an adjacent room as she waited for the doctor to come in.

When the doctor entered the room after what seemed an unusually long time, he chatted generally about how Patty was feeling and went on to explain that he had discovered some white spots on the baby's heart. It is common knowledge that women who are in their late thirties, as Patty was, have a higher chance of having a child with Down syndrome or some type of genetic challenge. White spots were an early indication that something was wrong in the baby's development. The doctor recommended additional testing to be sure. We asked, "What will the additional testing tell us? Is there a risk in doing the tests?" He answered that the tests would be able to identify the presence of any chromosomal abnormalities, such as Down syndrome. He added that, yes, there was a small risk—the baby could be hurt or even killed—in performing amniocentesis, a process in which the doctor draws amniotic fluid from the mom and baby by using a long, hollow needle stuck through the mom's abdomen and into the uterus. Miscarriage was also a possible result of the procedure.

Patty and I had arrived at the appointment full of the hope and happiness of expectant parents, and now we were left feeling anxious and even a little frightened for the future.

I felt sad and then angry at the doctor who knew so little about Patty and me that he simply assumed we would undergo further testing. If he had known a little bit more about where we were coming from, he might not have been so quick to recommend testing. He might have understood why we felt insulted by his strong insinuation that if we did find something wrong, we might decide to terminate Patty's pregnancy. He might have realized that we saw the baby as God's gift to us after having gone through ten years when Patty was unable to carry a baby full term. He might have appreciated the fact that finding out our baby would be a special child only served to make Patty, a protective mama bear, bond with her child even more.

Patty and I were both raised in religious households. A native of Montenegro, part of the former Yugoslavia, I was born into the Greek Orthodox faith. Patty was raised as a Catholic. After we were married, we were introduced to several Christian denominations, including Baptist and Presbyterian. We explored several of these and were excited by all of them, but we were especially captivated by the focus on faith and the sanctity of human life celebrated within Baptist and Presbyterian congregations. By the time Patty had become pregnant with our second child, we were regular churchgoers whose faith kept getting stronger and stronger.

The nine months of Patty's second pregnancy were busy ones for our family. We were planning to move to Florida to be closer to Patty's parents and soak up the sun. Growing up in cold climates—Patty in Minnesota and me in Montenegro and then the Bronx—had not endeared us to cold weather. We relished the idea of moving to a climate where our athletic and active family could spend more time outside. I was constantly traveling for my job as a sales consultant when a remarkable weekend with legendary college basketball coach John Wooden got me thinking hard about changing my career as well. Needless to say, our lives were busy and in a state of flux. It was a good, productive flux, but flux all the same.

Amid all of the changes, there was one thing we knew for sure: there would be no testing, and we were going to have this second child. The only question that remained was whether the doctor's concerns would show up when our child was born.

This would not be the last time the medical and health care communities would leave us feeling we had only two paths to choose from and that one of them would leave us pretty much on our own to fend as best we could.

What very few people knew, and our doctors certainly did not, was that my family and I had been fending for ourselves our whole lives, long before the twists and turns of life brought us to this doctor's office in Maryland. This book is the story of my family's journey up to that moment in Maryland, then beyond it, and up to the present. It is a journey that has taken on national—even international— interest after our son, Chris, whom the doctor had suggested we shouldn't have, made global headlines in 2020 and has inspired many people with his story, offering them hope and showing the power of perseverance and faith.

One note about how we are sharing Chris's story in this book. Although Chris and his accomplishments are the focus of *1% Better*, the text isn't in his voice. Down syndrome prevents him from communicating in this way all that has happened in his life. We are still very much coauthors, though, since Chris writes his story every day as he trains, competes, encourages others, and strives to get 1 percent better every day.

I'd never thought of my life as particularly remarkable— not until I started being asked to share it. Once Chris started on his inspiring journey, nothing could have prepared us for the wonders that took place within the Nikic family.

◆ ◆ ◆

Visit Panama City Beach IRONMAN Florida triathlon had been underway since before first light that morning, November 7, 2020. This was the only full distance IRONMAN triathlon offered in 2020; all other IRONMAN races had been shut down due to the COVID-19 pandemic.

The event took place against the backdrop of the Gulf of Mexico, and if you were going to swim, bicycle, and run for 140.6 miles, it was nice to know that you would never stray out of range of the breeze coming off the Gulf. Although it was before five o'clock and still dark out, the atmosphere that morning buzzed with the sounds and sights of athletes arriving and going through their warm-ups. Chris—along with Dan Grieb, Jennifer Sturgess, and Carlos Mendoza, members of the Central Florida Tri Club—began doing stretches as well. Dan was Chris's Unified partner and was responsible for Chris's safety throughout the event.

Chris had already achieved some notoriety by being the first person with Down syndrome to complete an Olympic triathlon and IRONMAN 70.3® triathlon. The Olympic triathlon comprises a 0.93-mile swim, 24.8-mile bike ride, and 6.2-mile run. The half distance and the ultra distance races are far more demanding than the Olympic distance. Those who have completed both IRONMAN triathlons say the ultra distance might be twice as long, but the half distance is five to ten times more difficult, especially mentally, to finish.

At any rate, as Chris, Dan, Jenn, and Carlos were doing their stretching, I noticed a small crowd gathering around them. It turned out that dozens of athletes were waiting to give Chris a hug and wish him luck. Everywhere Chris and Dan went, athletes stopped them to give Chris a hug. Others cheered or clapped as they walked by. Some wanted to pose with Chris for photos. Representatives from the IRONMAN Group, Special Olympics, and ESPN, plus a documentary filmmaker and local news channels, were all following them around and looking for an opening to interview Chris. When Dan and Chris went to check in Chris's bike, a fresh wave of well-wishers descended on them. Dan didn't want to be rude because he knew the well-wishers were genuinely rooting for Chris and wanted to do their part to spur him on to success, but they added to the pressure. The athletes try to build in some extra time before a race to give themselves a buffer, and Chris and Dan were forced to use every second of theirs.

The first event, the swim, involved two loops around the Russell-Fields Pier, which juts out into the turquoise waters of the Gulf. Each loop was 1.2 miles for a total of 2.4 miles. The athletes' official race time started at the water's edge when they entered the water. All the athletes received the traditional seventeen hours to complete the race (subject to intermediate cutoff times throughout the event).

Each of the three events offered its own special challenge for Dan and Chris. For the swim, Dan fixed a black bungee cord to Chris for added safety. This was a good thing because it turned out that Chris and Dan were allowed to go first. The problems with this arrangement, though, became immediately evident: they had no one to follow, and a kayak the event organizers had thoughtfully assigned to watch over them blocked Dan's sight lines to the guide buoys, which required Dan to execute a series of difficult and tiring maneuvers to keep on course. Another problem involved the hundreds of swimmers who would overtake Chris and run into him. To try to avoid the crowds, Chris and Dan took a longer path to stay out of the way, so they actually had to swim longer to avoid the crowds. Fortunately, by the second lap they had a nice rhythm and figured out how to finish on time.

During the bicycle leg, because Chris could not balance on his bike well enough to drink or eat while riding, every thirty minutes he had to stop and climb off his bike to hydrate. When he did that on mile 22, he found himself standing atop a large mound of red fire ants, which swarmed his ankles and bit at his flesh, causing his legs to swell. Dan jumped to the rescue and used his water bottle to wash Chris from stem to stern to get rid of the little red devils. Chris managed to get going again, but about halfway through the 112-mile ride, the course turned hilly, and Chris began going too fast to negotiate the winding, downhill turns. At a little piece of road that had once been sloppily repaired, Chris lost control of his bike and went into a long, ugly crash. Dan swerved around him and stopped twenty yards ahead, jumped off his bike, and ran back to the spot where Chris crashed. Dan found Chris standing there, laughing. "I just crashed my bike! I just crashed my bike!"

Chris was bruised and had a bloody knee, but he was in good enough shape to keep going. His sense of humor was intact, and so was his bike. However, mentally he was visibly shaken. For the next 30 miles, his speed slowed down from an average of fifteen miles an hour to about ten miles an hour. Between the time lost to ant bites, the bike crash, and now slowing down, Chris went from being thirty minutes ahead of pace to thirty minutes behind and at serious risk of missing the cutoff time. At mile 80, I met Chris and Dan to tell them that they were way behind and probably were not going to make the cutoff time unless Chris did something he had never done before. I pulled Chris aside, gave him a big hug, and said, "Hey, buddy, if you want to be an IRONMAN athlete today, for the last loop, you will need to ride faster than you have ever ridden before." He had 32 miles to go. I repeated the same question I always ask him: "What is going to win? Your 'fake' pain or your dreams?"

He said, "My dreams."

He made up the thirty-minute gap and finished with eight minutes to spare.

The marathon segment began with Chris stopping every few steps to give hugs to all the well-wishers gathered at the starting line. If there is one thing that motivates Chris, it is a hug. After this, Chris and Dan began looping through the streets of Panama City Beach in the nighttime darkness. Chris was again tethered to Dan so he would keep a steady pace to prevent going too fast or too slow. The two-loop course is filled with breathtaking views of the Emerald Coast waters along the shoreline. The run began in Aaron Bessant Park and went down to the shoreline to a little turnaround at Joan Avenue, then wound back the same way.

At mile 10 Chris began to slow so much that it seemed he was barely moving at all. As they say in endurance sport circles, Chris had hit the wall. Most marathon runners hit a wall at 20 miles, so hitting it at 10 miles was concerning. Dan tried several techniques to get Chris moving again, but nothing was working. So they called me, and I scootered out to meet them. Dan and I argued a little bit about the best way to bring Chris home to the finish line—I favored undoing the tether, but Dan disagreed. Ultimately it was my decision, and we removed the tether.

Before I left them to finish the race on their own, I pulled Chris to me and told him that there was a battle going on in his head between his fake pain—when continuing the race became uncomfortable—and his dreams.

"Who is going to win?" I asked.

Chris answered, "My dreams are going to win."

I said to Chris, "Okay, buddy, now it's time to put the

tether back on to help you keep a steady pace," and he agreed. Then I turned to Dan, Carlos, Jennifer, and Chris and said that God had sent angels to be with my son and I was going to trust that Chris's angels would bring him home. It was now Dan's call to finish the race with Chris in whatever way he deemed best. I trusted him as I would trust myself to see Chris through. I went on ahead to the finish line; they wouldn't see me again until they crossed it.

Once Chris found his rhythm, nothing could stop him. Chris and Dan made up so much time that, with two miles to go, Dan realized they could literally walk in the last two miles and stay under the time limit. After stopping for a few minutes to give hugs to his adoring fans, they chose instead not to slack off but to give it their all.

When the race began nearly seventeen hours earlier, it was still dark out. The dark had returned as thousands of athletes made their way over the 140.6-mile course, cheered on by the crowds and one another. At the finish line, where I stood with friends and family, many athletes had already finished the race, but the buzz began to grow as three figures came into view. Of course, I knew who they were: Chris and two older runners, Dan and Carlos.

As they crossed the finish line, Chris managed to raise his arms in victory as light bulbs flashed from hundreds of cameras and a roar went up from the crowd. What Chris had, in fact, just achieved was to become the first person with Down syndrome to complete an IRONMAN triathlon.

The newly christened IRONMAN athlete, Chris was, of course, the grown-up version of the unborn child my wife, Patty, and I had seen that Maryland doctor about some twenty years earlier. Now, here he was, crossing the finish line with arms held high in celebration and a little time to spare at 16 hours, 46 minutes, 9 seconds.

"Chris Nikic, you are an IRONMAN!" Mike Reilly, the voice of IRONMAN triathlons, shouted.

Later, after a medical check, his wounds were bandaged, and then Chris and his extended team went back to the house, put on recovery boots, and chowed down at Waffle House. Chris was in love with the world, and the world was falling in love with him.

Oh, and that dream he chose to follow rather than the pain? It was to be just like you and me: to be independent, get married, and share his life with someone he loves.

PART 1

1

FROM MONTENEGRO
TO THE BRONX

To understand our family and my relationship with Chris, and to put deeper context around his accomplishments, we have to go back to the old country where I was born and raised until the age of ten. When I was born in Montenegro, its population hovered around five hundred thousand, making it feel more like a sizable city than a country. My family lived on a farm in the southern part of Montenegro, near its border with Albania. My father had a fourth-grade education and traveled to Switzerland for three to six months at a time to work and send money back home. My mom took care of the farm and my brothers and me. She was the educated one of the pair, with an eighth-grade education. Despite working her fingers to the bone, my mom could only handle my two little brothers, so my parents sent me off to live with my grandmother until I was six years old.

I always felt loved by my parents, who provided us with a model of hard work and sacrifice that would give us the strength to overcome any obstacles we faced. My grandparents' farm was in the mountains against a backdrop that must have been beautiful. I was a child and can only recall spending most of the time with a friend I made there, getting into all sorts of trouble.

One of the best memories I have of that time was going into the barn where food—including pigs and cheese—was smoked. While poking around, my friend and I discovered large, wooden, saucer-shaped molds that were used to age cheese after it had been smoked. We found a dozen that didn't have cheese inside, so we took them to the hill where we used to sled. One at a time, we each sat on a saucer and sledded down the hill. Sometimes we'd hit a rock and split the saucer in half, but we'd just get another one and continue sledding.

By the end of the day, we had gone through all twelve of the molds. I got a pretty good whipping from my grandpa, but the day remains one of my fondest memories of the years I lived with my grandparents.

A second vivid memory from those years was being baptized in the Greek Orthodox Church. The baptism took place in the dead of a Montenegrin winter in the mountains, so you can imagine how cold it must have been. That didn't stop the priests from putting me in a large tub of cold water to be baptized. I remember watching the priests in their great black *kalimavkions*, moving solemnly toward me as I shivered naked in the water.

Once, when I had the worst toothache of my life—dentists were out of the question for us because my grandparents were too poor to afford the trip into town and the cost of a dentist—I desperately needed to get rid of the pain, so I went to my friend's uncle and asked him to pull my tooth out with a pair of pliers. He obliged. If you are thinking that this kind of upbringing made me tough, you are right. In some deep way I could not have understood, I learned that life brought both pain and joy and that certain actions produced certain consequences. There was no use complaining about those consequences because it wouldn't change a thing. Hard work and perseverance were what mattered.

Although my grandparents' farm was only about three hours from my parents' house, I never saw my parents between my fourth and sixth birthdays. Working in Switzerland, my father was able to make more money doing various types of manual labor, so after a couple of years, my parents saved enough money to have me move back with them. I rejoined my brothers and my parents when I was six years old and began school in the first grade.

My parents realized that I was a strong student. My mother was a tiger mom and pushed us to excel in academics. I vividly remember her telling me stories about how, someday, I would be an engineer and do respectable work and truly live the life I deserved to live. I'm not entirely sure why, but in the Montenegro of my youth, engineers seemed to hold the same kind of status among socially ambitious parents as doctors do in the United States. She knew of people who had graduated from university with a degree in engineering and had gone on to get well-paying jobs at big factories, which may have been miserable places to work for many, but the idea fired my imagination as a boy. I don't know . . . maybe I thought of factories as places with lots of white-coated scientists buzzing around and working the levers on huge machines, all while looking very important.

My dad was traveling a lot for work, so we hardly ever saw him. My mom was very young—still a teenager when she had three children—and didn't know how to be a mother. She was a strict disciplinarian who made sure I studied hard all the time, and she even helped me with some of my schoolwork. I have no doubt that if she'd had the same opportunities that I would go on to have in the United States, she would have become a very accomplished woman! She was loving and tough in the old-world sense. When my brothers or I did something we weren't supposed to do, she made us find a thin and flexible switch from a tree branch, pull off all the leaves and everything, and then give it to her. We would put out our hands, and she'd give us a couple of swats with it, burning our hands something memorable. And that was the point: we rarely committed the same misdeed twice. In hindsight, my mom wishes she never did this, but I'm glad she did.

One of my earliest memories of growing up involved watching my dad and his brothers and a couple of neighbors build a house for our family on the farm. They dug a hole for the foundation and then dug a second hole and filled it with rocks they gathered from around the mountainside. They cut down trees from the woods and built a huge bonfire, into which they placed the rocks and heated them to a melting point. The melted rock, collected in containers, became mortar for the bricks used to construct the house.

It was incredibly labor intensive, but our house was rather small, certainly no more than sixteen by ten feet. That's where the five of us lived: in this house with three spaces separated by sheets. One space was where my brothers and I slept. Another space was where my parents slept, and a third space was where we kept a woodstove oven for cooking and heat as we had no running water or electricity.

It's hard now to believe we lived like that. It's also hard to imagine how amazing my parents were—at such a young age they were able to raise us to accomplish what we have despite starting out so poor. I always tell people that when you grow up the way I did, nothing you experience later fazes you, so I am thankful for everything we have and the amazing life we live in this great country.

During the Cold War, the United States initiated a program for people who wanted to escape from Communist countries and emigrate to America. Today it all sounds like something from a spy novel, but the program enabled people who found themselves in non-Communist countries to get assistance obtaining a visa and a flight to the United States. The US government paid for the whole thing. My uncle had already participated in the program and was living in New York, so we knew it was legitimate and would work. My parents decided to take advantage of the program for our family.

Relocating was quite an adventure. On a warm May evening in 1970, our last night in our home, we went to bed and were awakened at ten o'clock by my father. He told us to get our things ready—the few clothes we had, a keepsake or two—and put them in the two suitcases my mother had packed. A little after ten, a car silently pulled up in front of our house. The five of us put our suitcases in the trunk and got in, and with the whole village asleep below us, we started our journey to freedom. The trip was a long one—about a twelve-hour drive. We slept in the car and arrived at the Austrian border around midday the following afternoon, having traveled far north from our farm in the southernmost tip of Montenegro. To this day, I wonder whether my parents concocted some kind of fake story about why we were traveling so far from home, just in case the authorities questioned them along the way. The kind of freedom to move around that we take for granted in America did not exist in what was then a part of Communist Yugoslavia.

The borders between European countries were relatively flexible, so the driver was able to take us across the border and all the way into Vienna. Since my dad had been working in Switzerland and other countries, he knew his way around foreign places and had arranged for us to rent an apartment in Vienna for a few months while we got our visas in order and bought airline tickets.

I recall the day we arrived at John F. Kennedy International Airport in New York City and I looked out the airplane window at the great swath of buildings that formed the city's skyline. The events of my family coming to America seem like they happened a lifetime ago. But I have come to see a direct connection to the spirit of courage my parents showed when, poor and utterly devoid of insider influence, they made their way through some treacherous territory in search of a better life for their children. As a child, I was more or less along for the ride. Now I see that their indomitability and perseverance furnished the moral fiber that I would draw on when I had to care for a family of my own.

My uncle met us at the gate—this, of course, was during the time when passengers could be greeted as they emerged from the plane. I remember bits and pieces of the car ride as we rode to his house: buildings going as far as I could see, a big bridge with cars streaming over it, and people everywhere. We stayed with my uncle and his family for a few days and then moved to an apartment they had found for us in the Bronx. Renewing my relationship with my cousins, whom I hadn't seen in years, was great. Our apartment included a bedroom for my parents, a bedroom for us three boys, and little kitchen and living room areas—modest but a big step up from a house with walls made out of bedsheets.

We had left Yugoslavia, gone to Austria, and finally arrived in the United States on October 21, 1970. I was ten years old. Back then, I never would have imagined that fifty years later I would have a son who would become the first person in the world with Down syndrome to participate in an IRONMAN triathlon.

My parents enrolled me in the fourth grade at our local public school, PS32. The first six months were a blur because I didn't speak a word of English. I sat in the back of the class, not really knowing what was happening and just trying to pick up the language through osmosis. A box full of Scholastic Reading Achievement cards, designed to help with reading and vocabulary, was available in our classroom. I devoured the entire box, and things started to come together for me. I remember being hungry to learn, so much so that in my first year I went from the lowest-achieving class to the highest. By the time I reached sixth grade, I was considered by teachers and classmates alike to be at the top of my class.

Before I entered junior high, the school administrators talked to my parents about having me skip the seventh grade and go directly to eighth. My parents, God bless them, told them that I wasn't that smart, so if the school was telling us to skip a grade, well, it meant the school wasn't operating right. My parents' solution was to send me to a Catholic school. The Catholic school took a little longer to adjust to because the teachers challenged me far more than my teachers at the public school had done. Still, by the time I graduated from the eighth grade, I managed to reach the top of the class again.

At that point, thanks to a combination of my hard work and my parents' financial shrewdness, my parents decided to pay the $2,500 annual tuition and send me to Fordham Preparatory School in the Bronx—a very nice high school. My parents both worked two full-time jobs so they could provide for our family. During the day, my dad was a maintenance man at an apartment building in Manhattan, and my mom had a night shift cleaning office buildings in that borough, so one of them was always home with us. Both of them acted as superintendents in the building where we lived in the Bronx. In exchange for taking care of the building, superintendents earned a small salary and a free apartment. Sometimes my brothers and I would help them with little projects around the building, like sweeping the stairs and hallways. The building had no elevators, so everybody used the stairs.

I was always a physically active kid growing up, and that didn't change when we moved from the farmland of

Montenegro to the public parks of the Bronx. I lived on Arthur Avenue, and the neighborhood had all kinds of great Italian markets and restaurants. It's still a nice neighborhood and even has a major university nearby, the Albert Einstein College of Medicine. I used to love to go to the neighborhood park and play handball, basketball, and soccer with the other kids. I was probably a little bit better at soccer than basketball because in Yugoslavia everybody played soccer, or "football" as we called it. By the time I got to high school, however, I was getting pretty tall, and I began to gravitate toward basketball more than soccer.

Growing up in New York City in the early 1970s had a rough-and-tumble quality. A fair amount of hostility existed between rival gangs divided by race or ethnicity. I personally saw many times when kids crossed one side of the street and were beaten up for being the wrong color or ethnicity. We lived in the Italian section, and, for some reason, there were a lot of Slavic immigrants. We were pretty much left alone, which was okay by my parents and okay by me. The Italians had their gangs, but they were very tolerant of those of us who had come over from Yugoslavia. We went to school together, played on the same sports teams, and even hung out at some of the same shops and cafés after school.

Maybe it was because my mom kept drumming into me that I was destined to be an engineer, but, fairly early in my life, I began thinking about how I was going to achieve that goal. By the time I reached high school, I realized that if I was going to become an engineer, I had to go to college. And if I wanted to go to college, I had to find a way to pay for it. My parents might have been able to come up with $2,500 for prep school, but I knew they couldn't possibly afford to pay $20,000 per year for college. I needed to find a way to get a scholarship.

I tell you the story about how I became a basketball player because it foreshadowed the work Chris and I would do later. In many respects I treated Chris's development as a triathlete in the same way I treated my development as a basketball player: the extreme pursuit wasn't done out of enjoyment so much as a means of achieving stated goals and dreams. My dream was to be successful and have a nice home and family. To realize that dream, I needed to hit my goal of being an engineer. Chris's dream, similar to mine, was to become financially independent, and he needed a big goal, like completing an IRONMAN race. It's interesting how people confuse dreams and goals. My dream and Chris's dream were almost identical, but we had very different goals for getting on the road to our dreams.

At the time, I was about six feet one and 125 pounds, soaking wet (as we used to say). It occurred to me that one way to earn a scholarship was to play a sport at a college where I could also study engineering. I knew other boys at my school who had earned athletic scholarships. Why couldn't I? I figured basketball was my best bet. I was the tallest boy in the class, and even though I couldn't play, I knew I could learn. Still a freshman, I took my proposal to Bruce Bott, the varsity basketball coach.

"Hi, coach," I said. "My name is Nik Nikic, and I really want to go to college. I need a scholarship to be able to go, so I want to get a basketball scholarship. Can you teach me to play?"

"Well, can you play at all now?" he asked.

I said, "No, not really, but I'll work hard and learn if you'll teach me. I'm a fast learner."

He had me dribble for a few seconds and take a couple of shots. I could tell from the look on his face that he was thinking whatever potential this tall, skinny kid had, I was going to be a special project.

"I'll tell you what I'll do for you," he said. "I live on Long Island and commute to school early every morning to beat the traffic. I usually arrive here before six o'clock, go for a run, and grab a shower before I start teaching. If you want, you can use the gym while I go running. We'll see what happens."

I took him up on his offer. I got up every day at five o'clock and walked twenty-five minutes to school. I would arrive at six o'clock at the gym, two hours before any of the other students arrived, and go through all the drills Coach Bott taught me. We had a beautiful gym located in the school's basement, with rubber floors and no windows. After school, I would put in another couple of hours. That year I made the freshman team. I didn't get to play very much, but I was learning the game. During the summer between my freshman and sophomore years, I kept the pressure on myself and would go to the park and practice for five or six hours every day.

By the time my sophomore year started, I'd distinguished myself as one of the top two players on the junior varsity team. With Coach Bott's permission and the help of the JV coach, Father Sullivan, I continued with the same routine of arriving early for practice, playing in the afternoon after school, and practicing all summer. In my junior year,

I became the only junior to start on the varsity team. In my senior year, we posted the best record in Fordham Prep's history, and I became a New York City high school all-star. It's amazing what you can accomplish when you feel there are no ifs, ands, or buts about what you have to do.

My senior-year success attracted some interest, and Father Sullivan eventually introduced me to a coach he knew at Johns Hopkins University, Jim Amen. Father Sullivan had taken a liking to me early on because of my work ethic. He was also an assistant to Coach Bott, so he followed my progress all through my high school years. Father Sullivan grew up in Baltimore, and his mom was still there, so when I began to look seriously at colleges, he recommended I consider Johns Hopkins, which is a world-class engineering and science school.

During my visit to the university, Coach Amen watched me shoot around and told me that as a Division III school, Johns Hopkins didn't offer sports scholarships, but I was fortunate to be able to earn enough grants and other funding to cover my entire undergraduate education. Well, that worked out just as well. I went to Johns Hopkins to play basketball and become an engineer. Goals are achieved when you are willing to work hard for them.

I owe Father Sullivan and Coach Bott a huge debt of gratitude for believing in me and assisting me in reaching my potential.

◆ ◆ ◆

At Johns Hopkins I was a four-year starter at shooting guard, despite consciously deciding to focus on academics and tone down the rigorous commitment to practice that helped me get into college in the first place. The truth was, I didn't go to college to play basketball; I went to get an education and fulfill my, or my mom's (I'm not sure which), vision of becoming an engineer. Because Johns Hopkins was an NCAA Division III university, I could get away with taking my foot off the gas with basketball, still contribute enough to be a starter, but not have to treat basketball as though it was a job. I liked basketball, but to me it was just a means to an end. Getting into Johns Hopkins to be an engineer was the real goal.

I graduated from Johns Hopkins with a degree in electrical engineering and computer science. As fate would have it, I was not destined to become an engineer after all, at least not right away. Eventually I did design software packages and apps, but out of school I chose to go into sales.

As I started my first after-graduation job at Fairchild Semiconductor in Poughkeepsie, New York, I felt that I had done my part in helping my parents' dreams come true. They were farmers who were used to hard work and after reaching America worked day and night as laborers to provide for my brothers and me. They showed us how to work hard and love our family. Within the span of a single generation, I was graduating from a world-class university with a job selling semiconductors to IBM.

Let me tell you about my amazing family. My mom and dad were married when he was twenty-five and she was fifteen. My mom was raised by a single mom, Aneta (I called her Mama), who lived with her parents during a very difficult time in the history of Yugoslavia. When my dad asked for my mom's hand in marriage, that was the end of school and her childhood. My mom is tall, athletic, smart, sweet, loving, and tough as nails. She has always been the rock of the family. My dad was the most loving, hardworking, and kind man you could ever meet. The two of them were amazing together and did what they had to do to give my brothers and me a chance at a better life.

Nothing was more important to my parents than my brothers and me. That was the greatest lesson I learned from my parents. So when people ask why I've dedicated so much time to helping Jacky and Chris, the answer is easy: I learned from my parents.

My two amazing little bothers, Peter (Zoro) and John (Goro), and I have different personalities and interests, but we are the same in the things that matter. We learned from our parents that family comes first. We also learned that nothing is given to you, so you have to earn it by working hard. We are all living the American dream. We all have relatively successful careers and are able to provide for our families. Peter went to Embry-Riddle Aeronautical University and became an engineer for the railroad but also built his own real estate business. John went to a two-year vocational school as a computer tech but quickly found his passion as a luxury custom-home builder in Westchester County, New York. Peter has been married for more than thirty years to his amazing wife, Fanda, and they have three beautiful kids—Marko, Bianca, and Anthony. John has been married for about twenty years to his equally amazing wife, Donna, and they also have three beautiful children—Ryan, Madison, and Aiden.

I am truly blessed with incredible parents and brothers.

2

WORK AND FAMILY

When I was in college, I asked one of my career counselors what I should do for work. He replied that it depended on what I wanted out of life. I thought for a moment and said that because I had been poor my whole life, I wanted to make a lot of money to support raising a family. I didn't want to be poor anymore.

"Well," he said, "with your engineering degree, if you can get into technical sales, you can make a boatload of money." That's why I pursued the track I did, even though I am rather introverted and freely admit that selling wasn't something that came naturally to me. I had only been on the job at Fairchild for six months when the company sent me to Minneapolis for a week of sales training. The training was routine for the company, but this particular trip was a life-changing event for me. The trainer was a man by the name of Jack Keenan, a smooth, articulate blond man who had earned a PhD in psychology. Dr. Keenan was just unbelievable. I had gone to the training to learn selling techniques but found myself fascinated by Keenan's teaching skills instead. He spoke so easily and persuasively and logically that I knew I wanted to learn to do that myself. Even more than that, I knew I wanted to be a teacher.

I suppose I felt a pang of regret at not having chosen to go into teaching and coaching in the first place. It was true, I admitted to myself, I certainly would not have been able to make nearly as much money as I could in sales. But maybe, if things worked out, I would be able to pursue teaching down the road. I filed teaching away in the back of my brain.

My trip to Minneapolis was life changing in yet another way. On Saturday, the last night we were there, some of the sales reps who were in the training decided to go out for a night on the town. We wound up at a place called Rupert's Nightclub, a classy place that included live music. I was sitting at one of the bar tables with some other people, and for some reason I was compelled to turn around and look toward the nightclub entry. This was a rather large nightclub, and the door was a hundred feet away, but I sat transfixed when the closest thing to an angel I could imagine walked in the door. She stood by the doorway with another woman, and a glow appeared to be hovering over her. She had slightly curly hair and a cute smile, and she was wearing a beige sweater, long skirt, and a pair of nice brown flats. She radiated wholesomeness. *Man, if God can make anything more perfect than that, I can't imagine how*, I thought.

I watched her a little as she made her way through the

nightclub and ended up coming over to where my colleagues and I were hanging out. Several other women were around talking to our group, and she asked one of them, "Hey, is this chair taken?"

I happened to be saving it for another girl I had been talking to, but I piped up and said, "Yes . . . it's yours!" She must have thought this was a bit cheeky because she flipped her hair, turned her back to me, sat down, and ignored me for about half an hour. Eventually the girlfriend she had come to the nightclub with got into a deep conversation with someone in our group, and I moved in with as much confidence as I could muster.

It turned out she was mildly annoyed at being made to pay the full eighteen-dollar cover charge even though she and her friend hadn't arrived until after eleven o'clock. We had a nice conversation and went out for an early morning breakfast with a group of five people.

Patty grew up in St. Cloud, Minnesota, and went to the University of Minnesota. She worked as a sales rep for the Prince Matchabelli line of perfumes, and her sales territory included Michigan and Ohio. After our meal I walked Patty out to her car, and we exchanged phone numbers and promised to keep in touch. That Sunday night I called her from Poughkeepsie, and her dad answered the phone. I asked for Patty without identifying myself first, which isn't proper phone etiquette. Her dad decided to take advantage of my little slip by asking whether I was her friend Peter. I said no. Then he asked if I was Paul, then John, and then I stopped him and introduced myself as Nik from New York.

Patty and I chatted a bit, and eventually I got around to

asking her if she'd had a good time the previous night. She told me that was a good question and her mom had asked her the same thing.

"What did you tell her?" I asked.

"Well, I told my mom that I met the man I'm going to marry," she said. Now, that was a hard line to follow up on! But since I had already fallen in love with her the moment I laid eyes on her, my heart started to flutter. God is great.

We continued to talk regularly on the phone and fell deeply in love. This was during the days when long-distance calls were very expensive. Our phone bill for one month was $400. We heard about flights from Minneapolis to LaGuardia Airport for $89 and realized it would be cheaper to visit each other than talk on the phone. It was crazy not to fly. So, on a Fourth of July weekend, she combined a visit to see her sister on Long Island with seeing me. I picked her up at the airport, and we spent the whole weekend together. I took her to my parents' house, where my mom cooked her an amazing meal. I met her sister. The following weekend she came back to New York. The next weekend I went to Minneapolis for my one-week vacation to get to know her and her family.

During our courtship, Patty and I talked about the kind of family we wanted to have. I had two brothers, and she came from a family with five children. We thought that four children sounded about right. We also talked about religion and decided to have a Catholic wedding.

After six weeks had passed from our first date, I was flying to California and wanted to stop by Minneapolis for a visit. We talked about getting engaged and even went out and looked at some churches. During that stay, I asked her father for permission to marry his daughter, and his response was, "How are you going to provide the lifestyle she is accustomed to?" That was a tough question coming from one of the most successful oil distributors in the Midwest.

I said, "I will be a successful businessman, just like you."

He said, "Are you sure? Because there is no take back. In our family, marriages are permanent."

I said that was true in my family, too, so he gave me his blessing, and I proposed to Patty. She spent the next couple of months of our engagement planning the wedding, then came out to live in New York, renting a house from a woman I knew at IBM. We were married June 21, 1986, and have been happily married and in love ever since.

◆ ◆ ◆

The following years were busy ones for us. I moved to a different company, NEC Corporation, where I continued to work in sales. Two years into this job I was promoted to district sales manager, with distributors and engineers directly reporting to me. In August 1989, during our six months based on Long Island, Patty gave birth to a baby girl. We named her Jacqueline, Jacky for short. We immediately moved to Souderton, Pennsylvania, which is just northwest of Philadelphia, and lived there for two years.

One day I came home and said to Patty, "I have some good news and some bad news. Which do you want first?"

Patty wanted the good news. "I have been promoted to run the IBM global account team!" I announced.

"And the bad?" asked Patty.

"We have to move back to Poughkeepsie." Patty was not a huge fan of the city, but I promised her we would have to stay in Poughkeepsie for only a year and a half tops. It turned out we lived there for nearly four years.

◆ ◆ ◆

In January 1990, Patty and I had been on a plane and happened to sit next to a man who was a lawyer. I am not generally chatty and am even less so on planes, so he engaged her in conversation. Eventually I found myself drawn into the conversation and mentioned that I was interested in starting my own business someday. The man replied that he might have an opportunity, and I should contact him at his home in Florida. During that trip, we were visiting Patty's parents in Fort Myers and decided to go to Orlando for a couple of days before returning home. On our way to Orlando, we stopped to meet with our new acquaintance, David, his wife, Camille, and their two young daughters. I saw a successful businessman, an amazing family, and a lifestyle that I didn't even dare to dream of having. He introduced me to the Amway plan, a business model that built a multibillion-dollar company through direct sales of various health, beauty, and home care products. The company follows a multilevel marketing system that allows individuals to build their own network of independent distributors and earn commissions.

I started building my Amway business in my spare time that year while staying focused on my career. Within the two-and-a-half-year period that I ran the IBM team at NEC, we grew our revenue from $30 million to $550 million. As for

Amway, Patty and I worked together to build up a wildly successful business. In addition to bringing in income, Amway provided a learning system of books, tapes, and seminars that helped me develop my sales and presentation skills. Part of my role as the outward-facing part of our team involved making presentations to rooms full of prospective recruits. I poured myself into practicing my techniques for public speaking, which does not come naturally to me. Eventually we built an almost ten-thousand-person networking business.

I was working my tail off between being full-time at NEC and part-time with Amway, putting in more sixteen-hour days than I care to remember. When my income from my part-time business exceeded my full-time career, I decided to quit the corporate world and focus part-time on my business while looking for my next career move. I noticed most of the other Amway leaders all had other business ventures.

After I left NEC, Patty and I wanted to celebrate the beginning of a new chapter in our lives by buying a forty-foot motorhome and taking a six-month tour of the country along with Jacky, who was six years old at the time. We had a wonderful time. We then moved from Poughkeepsie to Westminster, Maryland, a wonderful town where the weather was much better.

After a year of playing lots of golf and getting bored, I began to look seriously into what I was going to do next. I had accomplished my goal of making a lot of money and wanted the next chapter to involve something meaningful. I thought about it for a while and then came up with a terrific idea: I would call Jack Keenan, the sales training consultant who had captivated me in Minneapolis, and renew our acquaintance.

I told him how much I had enjoyed being a part of his class in Minneapolis and that I wanted to learn to do what he did and wondered if he could offer any advice. It turned out that Keenan was a representative for a sales methodology company called OnTarget based in Atlanta. He sponsored me to get certified to teach the class he was selling. And just like that, I was pivoting to a new career.

OnTarget sold a strategic opportunity management class that many of the largest companies used to train their sales forces. I began to teach the same class that Keenan sold and taught. I traveled around the country, teaching salespeople in all kinds of businesses. My first class was with FedEx in Memphis. OnTarget always asked attendees to evaluate their instructors at the end of each class. I was told that my score was among the highest they had ever received. My success teaching these sales classes was in large part due to the skills I had learned doing seminars for Amway. I was able to refine my presentation skills and even managed to include some fun, an approach that always went over well with participants.

In my first year with OnTarget, I became a highly sought-after speaker. But I still thought of myself as being between jobs. I had achieved my goal of emulating one of my mentors, Jack Keenan, but I was never going to earn enough in this particular line of teaching. I kept my ear close to the ground for something new.

That something new materialized when it occurred to me that somebody had to be selling OnTarget's programs to all of these big organizations with gargantuan training budgets. "How does it work?" I asked a colleague. It turned out that the company contracted commissioned agents, like Jack, who received 25 percent of everything they sold. Well, that was very interesting and certainly a much better-paying job than teaching the classes themselves.

I went to the owners and said, "I would like to be one of your agents." OnTarget knew who I was because many of their more successful agents were booking me to teach their classes. Still, they put me off at first even though the job was a commission-only salary structure. Eventually they gave in, and I went on to become their top new account closer, which included bringing in clients such as Xerox, EMC Corporation, Deloitte & Touche, and other huge accounts. Between my work with OnTarget and Amway, I was working hard, teaching classes, and working with Patty on having a second child.

◆ ◆ ◆

One of the most important outcomes of the work Patty and I did with Amway came in January 1999, when we hosted a convention in Tampa, Florida. The keynote speaker for the event was basketball coach John Wooden. As a reward for being some of the fastest-growing distributors, Patty and I were blessed to be chosen to act as Coach Wooden's chaperones for the entire weekend. Soccer may have been my native sport, but basketball was my adopted sport in America. If you grew up in 1970s America and learned to play basketball and love the game, you knew who John Wooden was: the coach of the most successful basketball program of all time, winning ten national championships with the UCLA Bruins during a twelve-year period. People thought of him as the consummate winner, a stern and wise yet reticent fatherly figure who could manage the adolescent egos of elite athletes, such as Lew Alcindor (Kareem Abdul-Jabbar) and Bill Walton.

Most sports fans knew of Coach Wooden's record of accomplishment, but fewer knew about the mindset and habits that made him successful, which he generously shared with his players and those he mentored. He believed that success was less about strings of championships or impressive numbers and more about the little masterpieces you constructed from the improvements you made every day.

I certainly didn't know about this deeper aspect of the man when I saw him making his way out of the Jetway clutching a single, small carry-on. "Do you have any other luggage?" I asked.

"No, this is it. I travel light," said the great man. Of course he did.

We took him to his hotel so he could relax a little bit and change. Then we went to the hall where he was to deliver his speech. It seems a little strange to say it now, but I don't recall the contents of the speech he made that day as clearly as I do our conversation over dinner that evening. At the restaurant, I did what many had probably done before, asking him some specific questions about his favorite teams and players and years. I had played college ball and felt a kinship with him. I was in heaven listening to him talk about how great the players were and what they could do as well as how wonderful they were as human beings. I could tell from the way Coach Wooden spoke about his players that this mattered a lot to him. He told us a story about the great UCLA center Bill Walton, who led the Bruins to national championships in

1972 and 1973, including helping put together an amazing eighty-eight-game winning streak.

Wooden was a very clean-cut person and believed that people should carry themselves with humility as well as confidence. One of the ways he implemented this philosophy was by demanding that his players wear their hair shorter than was fashionable during those tumultuous years. He also banned facial hair. The strong-willed Bill Walton, who fully embraced the sixties counterculture and loved to follow the Grateful Dead, insisted that he be allowed to keep his long locks and beard. "He said to me, 'Coach, I am convicted about this. I need to stand by my principles, and my hair and beard are a part of this,'" Wooden told us. "I looked at him and said, 'I completely understand, Bill. I'm all for it and think it's wonderful. We're going to miss you, Bill.'"

Somewhere along the way we got to talking about winning or success, and Coach Wooden noted how fixated most people are on results, such as the number of games or championships he won. He told us it took him many years before he began winning regularly and even more time before he won his first championship. If his career had taught him anything, he explained, it was that excellence takes a long time to become a habit. "It takes a long time to figure everything out. You have to be patient and focus on modifying things a little bit at a time. But if you can do that, then momentum picks up, and you just get smarter and better all the time." He added, "If you look at my progress over a short period of time, like thirty days, you don't see much. But if you look at it over two to three years, you see major improvements that build on one another." Then he concluded, "Be patient.

Success takes time and must be done with small, gradual, incremental changes."

I had always thought about my own life in terms of building a legacy, a great body of work that would represent all the little things I'd done to be successful. But Wooden wasn't concerned with bodies of work. He was focused on the honor and dignity of how you live your life and do your work, all culminating in the sacred ideal of making yourself a little better every day. A person didn't forget meeting John Wooden, and I certainly never forgot his words. They would form the bedrock of my teaching and coaching philosophy as a business consultant and as a father determined to help save his son from a life of isolation, neglect, and decline. For our family, the 1% Better concept and practice that I later developed would always be inspired by a remarkable man named John Wooden.

3

CHRIS IS BORN

As I noted in the introduction, Patty has had challenges with fertility and spent more of her adult life than she wanted to undergoing various treatments. Two miscarriages had not deterred us from wanting to have a second child, but the constant fertility treatments with no success were making her tired and frustrated. So in 1998 she told me she needed to give her body a break and stop seeing her fertility specialist for a little while. We talked about adopting. But in early 1999 she decided to resume her therapy, which meant that she had to undergo some monthly blood testing before starting the new fertility series.

We had recently returned from the Amway meeting in Tampa when our nurse called as Patty and Jacky were having breakfast in the kitchen. "I wanted to tell you that your blood test came back positive for pregnancy," the nurse said. Patty was speechless and told the nurse she would call her back.

As Patty hung up the phone, Jacky, who was nine years old at the time, said, "I think you're pregnant." I was traveling, and when Patty called me and told me she was pregnant, I was just as shocked as she was. And then shock turned to joy.

Things began to move fast at that point for us. Although we had been in the Northeast for most of our married life, we loved Florida. Patty's parents had retired to a home on a golf course in Fort Myers in 1986, and we went down there several times a year to visit. After one such visit we thought, *Why are we still up here in Maryland? Why aren't we living down there?* I could do my work living anywhere along the East Coast, so we decided to check out several cities and landed on Orlando. Patty was five months pregnant with Chris when we closed on a house and moved to Florida. Before we left, however, Patty went to see her Maryland doctor one last time for an ultrasound. That was when we received the news that our unborn child was going to have a different life than other kids. It was also when we knew we were going to go on that journey with him.

Chris was born October 6, 1999. The first thing I noticed about him was that he looked so small. I'm six feet six, and Patty is five feet ten, so we assumed Chris would be pretty big as well. He weighed only a little over five pounds, which was half the amount of his sister's birth weight. He had cute, tiny ears and looked like a baby monkey. I even called him our little monkey when he was born, and I still call him that today.

The doctors rushed him away to run tests, but we knew

right away that he had Down syndrome. Those almond-shaped eyes were unmistakable. The doctors were gone for a while, and when they returned, they told us Chris had Down syndrome as well as a VSD, a ventricular septal defect—basically a hole in his heart. They couldn't operate yet because he was too fragile, so we spent an extra day in the hospital just to allow Patty and Chris to stabilize.

Before we left, one of the doctors who had done the blood work on Chris came in to debrief us about our child. His bedside manner was terrible as he outlined all of the things that we could expect to happen or, in Chris's case, expect not to happen. We would be able to call ourselves very fortunate if Chris could learn to tie his shoes, he said. Chris would always be dependent on us for everything. He could never hold down a job or live any place by himself. If we could afford this option, we'd probably want to consider institutionalizing him at some point. Whatever dreams we had formulated for our child should be abandoned. Why torture ourselves with hopes that could never come true? If anybody wanted an object lesson in how to devastate somebody, that doctor would be the ideal tutor. I couldn't wait to get out of there.

Once we got home, we entered what I call our week of sadness and mourning over the son we had dreamed about but would never have. Like my mother, I had always been driven by a type A personality, overcoming any obstacle in my path. It wasn't difficult for me to conjure up images of my equally high-achieving son. After all, Jacky had already set the pace: she had started walking at nine months.

It's pretty easy in youth sports to tell who the naturally

gifted athletes are. They're quicker, more agile, and more aggressive. Before they are taught a single thing, they come by a dribble or shot or pass better than the others. Even at a young age, they play the game differently than the average kid. That was Jacky.

Like many kids today, Jacky played youth soccer and used to fly up and down the field. She played Amateur Athletic Union (AAU) basketball at a young age and ran track and threw the discus in junior high school. She was so physically gifted that she made the junior varsity track team as a thirteen-year-old middle schooler. The varsity coach brought her up to the varsity level to bolster the team in the early stages of the state tournament. She made it to the state regionals, and she set a record for her high school in the girls' discus throw that stood for years. She did all of this as a thirteen-year-old. And she did this with next-to-no form, no training, and no coaching; she just hauled up and heaved the thing farther out than any girl ever had at her high school. She is also smart as a whip and worked hard enough in school to wind up going to an Ivy League university and becoming a Division I athlete.

I imagined Chris being in this mold, a six-foot-nine male version of Jacky (and me) to whom I would impart my work ethic and skills in endless backyard one-on-one games. He would become this amazing specimen who went on to play basketball and be a leader on his team as well as in the classroom. I would even teach him to become an NBA player. (In addition to my confidence in my teaching skills, I had my recent meeting with John Wooden always in my mind.) Best of all, I could give Chris the benefit of all the things I didn't have growing up poor in Montenegro. That was probably going to be the sweetest thing of all, right? What parent doesn't want his child to have more than he did growing up? What parent doesn't want his child to be all he can be—to be better than him at something?

And then, of course, when a parent learns that a child has Down syndrome, those feelings, which are an important part of his own identity as a parent, as much as any identity the child will have, all go away. What was I left with? At first, a powerful sadness that left me lying on the bed with my arm over my eyes, crying. But, gradually, mourning over the son I didn't have turned into something quite different: acceptance of and love for the beautiful baby I did have. It wasn't long before the three of us started falling in love with our little Chris. I think Patty was always there, but I was right behind her.

Jacky had always told us that she wanted a little brother to play with, so when Chris was born, she was all over him. One of our family pastimes is playing dominoes. It took several years and a lot of therapy before Chris could take part in the games, but when he finally did, Jacky loved to torment him, as any big sister would. Chris was always very competitive, and when he played with just Patty and me, he would invariably twist the rules to be sure he came out on top. When Jacky played, she quickly became wise to Chris's ways and loved to sabotage the pieces. One of Chris's little quirks is that he likes things to be straight. This includes dominoes. Jacky used to set the games up with as many twists and turns as she could, leaving Chris helpless.

"They're too crooked," he would say, and then he'd fix her with a good look before straightening out the pieces.

For as long as I can remember, Jacky has also been fiercely

protective of Chris. There were times when Jacky was in high school that I had to talk my little alpha daughter down from exacting revenge on a classmate who had made a disparaging remark about Chris. "They're not worth the trouble," I tried to assure her.

Yes, we were a bit uncertain of what the future would hold. Even as we understood that Chris would miss out on some things, Jacky, Patty, and I had the fire in our bellies to make his life the best it could be. We needed to support one another unequivocally because we were not going to get support from anywhere else. Even some family members thought it was likely Chris would have to be institutionalized. I remember Patty and I having conversations in which we assured them, in no uncertain terms, that Chris was going to be a vital part of our family. "He's going to surprise us. You'll see!" we'd say. I think both Patty and I wanted to prove them wrong but also to dispel the doubts lurking in our minds as well. We are both stubborn people.

◆ ◆ ◆

When Patty and I got married, we talked about what we wanted things to be like when we had a family—who would be the primary breadwinner and who would be the primary caregiver for the kids, that sort of thing. We decided that I would earn the money and she would build a loving home. This was an arrangement that Patty very much wanted for herself. It was an arrangement that was perfect for me since I am by nature a workaholic, much like my parents. We didn't follow this arrangement with absolute strictness. From the beginning, for example, Patty and I both worked on the Amway business, with me as the face of our business and Patty on the administrative side of it and both of us participating in and delivering seminars.

Jacky was remarkably independent, so with her as our only child, it was easy for Patty to find time for our business. But with Chris in the picture, Patty was no longer able to work with me on Amway. When I wasn't flying all over the place on business, I was driving all over the place with Jacky for her AAU basketball games. Sometimes tournaments ran several days with overnight stays. Chris was going to be a full-time job for Patty, and probably a good deal more than that. After Chris was born, like Patty, I began to slowly disconnect from the rest of the Amway organization and the people we had grown to care about. It was a source of not only income but also our social life as we had made many friends within the company.

I had started my own consulting business and began putting together training programs of my own. In 2003 I launched the company, and we drifted away from our Amway business. Our relationship with the organization had been a positive one that allowed us to meet many wonderful people, whose friendship helped to renew our faith in God. We became financially secure enough for me to venture out on my own and combine my passions for sales and teaching as a corporate consultant. It also enabled us to have the resources we needed to meet the many and varied needs that would arise in raising a boy like Chris the way we believed he should be raised. The Amway business had turned out to be an amazing way to make friends and learn life skills. Now it was time to get working on the next chapter of our lives.

4

TOO WEAK TO NURSE

After Chris was born, Patty and I learned everything we could about Down syndrome. We each had vague ideas that it involved a chromosomal abnormality, and both of us had only indirect experience with it. One evening after Chris was born, we were talking about the subject, and Patty told me a story. When she was growing up, she knew a boy named Jerry who was different than the other kids. He was heavyset and walked with a loose stride. His eyes were almond shaped. He had Down syndrome. When she was growing up, boys like Jerry were hurtfully referred to as "retarded" and generally shunned by most people. Patty met Jerry when she began spending time with her grandmother on days when she went to kindergarten. The school lasted for a half day, after which her grandmother would pick her up and have a little outing, maybe lunch or a visit to church.

Patty and her grandmother started visiting the local senior citizens' home, the Little Sisters of the Poor, and doing volunteer work. One of the things Patty did was to team up with the grandson of her grandmother's friend, who was a resident of the senior citizens' home. The two of them would open a box of cookies and spread them on a tray along with bottles of water and take them around and offer them to the residents who were sitting in one of the common areas, such as the living room. Patty's teammate was Jerry.

Patty remembered being uncomfortable with the way people treated Jerry. Even his grandmother seemed to behave with a mean spirit toward him. Even though she was only five years old, Patty promised herself that if she ever had a son like him, she would be nice to him. After the geneticists confirmed to us that Chris had Down syndrome, Patty remembered Jerry and said quietly to herself, "Okay, thank you, Lord. Now, it's my turn to mother a son."

It was in this spirit that Patty made Chris the main focus of her life. We had chosen not to have Patty undergo an amniocentesis because we thought it might harm the baby or cause her to miscarry and because we felt committed to having the baby no matter what. In choosing this path, we left ourselves with no time to prepare to deal with Chris's disability. Neither Patty nor I regretted our decision, but she understood she had a lot of catching up to do, including reading and researching online. Early intervention is critical in the success and progress of someone with Down syndrome for reasons that soon became all too clear to Patty.

Down syndrome most often occurs during a process called nondisjunction, in which the two copies of chromosome 21 fail to separate during the formation of the egg, resulting in an egg with two copies of the chromosome. When this egg is fertilized, the resulting baby ends up with three copies of chromosome 21 in each of its cells. The cause of this nondisjunction remains unknown. Most people readily recognize the presence of Down syndrome by its visible effects: the smaller-than-average head, slanted eyes, and a soft and heavyset build, along with some other characteristics. The truth is there is no single look to those with Down syndrome, just as there is no single look to other kids. And just as there is no single look, there is also no single level of cognitive or physical function or capacity for development as the child matures. But there is no question that children born this way are far behind the developmental eight ball compared to other children. Getting them out from behind without delay offers the best, and only, way to help the child maximize key developmental years.

For us, there was no time to waste.

The minute she got home from the hospital, Patty ordered books about raising a child with Down syndrome. One of the best of them was *No Easy Answers: The Learning Disabled Child at Home and at School,* written by Sally Smith. Down syndrome is all about our five senses—the sense of touch, vision, hearing, smell, and taste. Children with Down syndrome are deficient in some or all of these senses. Patty quickly discovered that her top priority was going to be opening up those senses so that they developed at the highest possible levels they could. Developing Chris's senses was a critical first step in developing his cognitive ability as well.

Getting nourishment for Chris proved to be extremely

difficult. Chris had a "low tone" from head to toe, which meant that his muscles were floppy and hard for him to move. This also meant that he had very poor control in his cheeks, lips, and tongue, making it hard for him to nurse. To overcome his low tone, Patty connected with an oral motor therapist who taught her the physical exercises she would need to do with Chris. These exercises were as basic as putting on latex gloves and manipulating Chris's mouth, stretching his lips and cheeks from inside his mouth, trying to develop his tone so he would be able to suck in nourishment. She had a very challenging time getting Chris to nurse. Often during a nursing session, he would be overcome with fatigue and simply fall asleep. Patty believed this was because his heart was working so hard for so little nourishment. There was definitely not a quick fix. The oral motor skills are so vital to growth that Patty had to work with Chris on them for the first twelve years of his life.

When Chris was five months old, he still weighed under ten pounds and clearly was not thriving. We became very worried. Patty took him to see a cardiologist who told us that Chris needed surgery right away. Orlando did not have a neonatal cardiology group that performed surgeries, but about four months earlier, a group of cardiologists from around the country had relocated to set up a practice in Orlando.

A baby's heart at five months is the size of a walnut, so finding a surgeon who has previously worked with patients this young and this small is vital. I tend to be very respectful around doctors, but Patty had enough experience with them to be more comfortable being very direct. We set up a meeting with one of the cardiologists in the new group to talk about Chris.

"How many surgeries like this one have you performed?" Patty asked the doctor.

"More than six hundred to date," he replied.

"Have you ever lost anyone?" Patty continued.

"No, not a one."

That was all Patty needed to hear. On March 5, 2000, Chris had open-heart surgery. While performing the surgery, the doctor discovered that Chris had not one ventricular septal defect but two. The little guy had truly been fighting for his life during those five months, trying to grow healthy with two holes in his heart. The doctor also gave Chris a pacemaker that would be activated in case his heart didn't work well on its own. After seven days, as the doctors saw irregularities in Chris's heart, they said there was zero chance his heart would ever work on its own, so they would need to implement a permanent pacemaker. We begged them to give Chris one more day, and we called on our thousands of friends in Amway to pray for him. We were up all night praying for Chris's heart to heal.

The next day, the eighth day since surgery, the doctors came in to implant the permanent pacemaker. We asked them to test Chris one more time. They said there was no reason to test him again because there was no chance he wouldn't need the pacemaker. Period. End of discussion. But not for us. We persisted with our plea until they relented and agreed to a final test.

They tested him one more time and said they didn't understand what they were seeing—everything was fine with Chris's heart. It was beating by itself, and he would not need the pacemaker after all. But we understood: God had a vision for Chris and performed a miracle. God could see a future for Chris that we could not see. He needed a strong and healthy heart so he could one day enter an IRONMAN triathlon. Since that day, our faith in God has never wavered.

After the surgery Chris's body seemed to flip a switch to the On position. His energy level improved, and he grew much more assertive on the bottle, which Patty had switched to so he would be sure to get enough milk. He started to do better and gain some weight.

Patty's parents came up from Fort Myers to stay with Jacky, who was spending most of her time in school while Patty and I were in the hospital with Chris. Patty and I would take turns and go home to grab a shower or nap. The nurses kept urging us to hold Chris for long periods. Patty stroked his forehead and talked to him but was reluctant to hold him because he was hooked up to all sorts of wires and monitors and looked so fragile.

When Chris returned from the hospital, Patty went right to work again, helping him develop better use of his senses and motor function. One of their daily rituals involved giving Chris a bath, during which Patty massaged him from head to toe, kneading and stretching his cheeks, fingers, legs, arms, tummy, and back, all the while playing some music and talking to him to stimulate his mind and make the sessions more fun. After this, she dressed Chris and tried to feed him solid foods, which was very challenging because his frenulum—the piece of skin that attaches your tongue to the bottom of your mouth—was very tight and inflexible. If you think about the tongue, you realize how important it is to the whole process of eating as well as to our speech patterns and even in our thinking. It's a very important muscle that is almost constantly in motion, so Chris spent a lot of time learning to work it.

Visually, Patty gave Chris all sorts of things to explore around the house. I would come home from work and see Post-it notes attached to chairs, the refrigerator, the stove, drawers, toothpaste tubes, and just about everything you could imagine, all with big words spelled out for Chris to learn to vocalize. Patty also began to take him to a physical therapist to teach him some large-motor skills. Most parents don't have to teach their children to crawl. In one session, the therapist put Chris on his stomach and began helping him move his arms and legs, all while keeping his torso flat on the table. Over time he learned to inch up onto his hands and feet at the beginning of a rudimentary crawl. The therapist had all kinds of ingenious little strategies to slowly build motor muscle. We also had to learn and teach Chris sign language for a few years because his speech was delayed.

When I say *slow*, I do mean that progress was slow. I've always thought that Patty was one of the most patient people I've ever known, but Chris required patience on a whole new level because with Down syndrome everything is about repetition. When I was home, I watched her in action with Chris, having him repeat a word thirty, forty, or fifty times before he said it correctly. He had an outpatient surgical procedure on his tongue to create greater flexibility and allow him to develop more complex speech patterns. Patty took Chris in for oral motor therapy, where the therapist would make a game of having Chris learn to blow a cotton ball across the table. First, Chris used his mouth to blow the ball, and then he did it by using a straw, which made him have to work hard to pinch his lips together and blow enough air.

Patty also took Chris to an occupational therapist to learn how to apply his slowly developing motor skills to daily tasks such as eating. This involved exercises like putting him in a high chair with yogurt on the tray and letting him explore it, touch it, and play with it to understand its texture and taste.

Even the healthiest children get ear infections, but with Chris these were more frequent and difficult to alleviate. Patty did everything she could to keep him healthy, but he had to have three surgeries on his ears during his childhood. Patty and Chris spent a great deal of time together during his first sixteen years, but she and I also found plenty of time to be together, going for walks or going out to dinner or our weekly date nights.

Patty also hired someone to care for Chris when she needed to go to the grocery store or the hardware store or just needed a break, a little downtime from focusing on Chris twenty-four seven. The caregiver, Yvonne, had two children in the local middle school and had emigrated to the US from Colombia. Yvonne and Patty connected right off the bat. We also expanded our support network by becoming active in the Down Syndrome Association of Central Florida, which sponsored monthly meetings that Patty often attended. These meetings were wonderful because we could meet with other parents who were going through the same things we were. They mentored us, answered our questions, and offered empathetic shoulders to lean on.

The association was a great networking resource as well, a place to hear about good therapists and education programs and so on. We had potlucks and asked members to bring their families along, which created a very positive, encouraging environment. We were fortunate to live in a large city. A family living out in the country would have difficulty finding access to a robust group like ours. Patty became very close with a few of the moms whose children were five to ten years older than Chris. She learned a lot from them about what she would need to prepare for in the future.

From an economic standpoint, we were very fortunate to be able to pay for Yvonne's help and all the various specialists who worked with Chris. The local and state governments offer intervention services for families of children with Down syndrome for the first three years of the child's life. While helpful, this assistance is not nearly enough to overcome the disabilities targeted by the therapies.

Patty had the patience to deal with the insurance companies that were sometimes unwilling to pay for what we thought were basic types of therapies. With a curious mind and love for her son, Patty became an expert on Down syndrome, including its wide-ranging symptoms and therapies. Even more than this, however, she learned how to apply a mother's love to become an expert on a unique individual named Chris. I have often heard her tell people that Chris teaches her as much as she could ever teach him.

5

SCHOOL AND SPORTS

Y ou could argue our belief was misplaced, but both Patty and I had high expectations for Chris in terms of what he would be able to learn and how independent he could one day become. Florida has an early prekindergarten program that begins at three years old, so we enrolled Chris. Probably the best thing that came out of that experience was meeting a teaching assistant named Leigh. She became one of the sitters and was with us for a good ten years while Chris was growing up. From the start Chris took a real shine to Leigh. If Patty and I wanted to go out golfing or head out for the day, she would come over for four or five or six hours. Patty created a flowchart of Chris's daily activities, and Leigh would go over it with him while we were away. These included physical therapy, occupational therapy, music therapy, and behavioral therapy because Chris needed to learn how to behave if he was going to attend a school and be successful.

Chris needed a lot of help with behavioral therapy. He had a difficult time sitting still for more than a few seconds. At the therapists' offices, Patty used to take copious notes that she would apply later at home since it was impossible to see improvement in Chris with just a couple of visits each week. Leigh was wonderful. She understood the terminology written down in the book and how to apply it. After two years Chris's school principal retired, and we left as well. We learned that the principal sets the tone for the school, including the extent to which they promote inclusion. It was time to look for another school.

We went to sign Chris up for kindergarten and also attended some of the special education classes offered at the new school. This was a class AAA school, which meant that its students did very well on their national achievement exams. We were initially turned down for admission but went to mediation and prevailed, so we anticipated a little rockiness in the beginning. On Chris's fourth day of school, Patty wanted to check in and see how things were going. Patty sat off to the side as the teacher and students formed a circle and began to practice the alphabet. After this, they started practicing numbers, and the teacher would pick a student who had to say the number that came after the previous student's number. After the student next to Chris said "six," the teacher pointed to Chris, who said "nine."

The teacher said, "No, that's wrong." Not, "Close, Chris, but the next number is seven." Just "that's wrong." And then she pointed to the next student.

Patty immediately stood up and went over to the circle and, before the entire class, said to the teacher, "Excuse me, but what was that? You were given a teaching moment, and you chose, instead, to disrespect my son." And she took Chris by the hand and stormed out of the room and headed straight to the principal's office. She informed the principal that we could not stay at a school that did not embrace our child. A child cannot succeed if he is not embraced. "If the teacher behaved this way with me sitting ten feet away," Patty said, "I can only imagine her treatment of Chris when I am not there."

At another school we tried, we experienced the opposite problem: the teacher was very warm and doted on Chris but couldn't bring herself to set expectations for him. So we went to a different school. We continued to try out schools to find the right fit. At one of them, the teacher seemed fine, but the students bullied Chris and wrote hurtful things on his artwork. We did a lot of positive talking to buoy Chris up while we continued our search. Thanks to a tip from our friends in the Down Syndrome Association, we heard about an international school where students spent two days a week in the classroom and two days homeschooling. This worked out well for Chris, who was able to focus on his phonetic language skills. I could tell Patty was enjoying working side by side with Chris and witnessing the light bulbs going off when he grasped a subject.

On the days he was in the classroom, it was good for Chris to be with other students and figure out how to model himself after them, observing how they interacted with one another and their teachers. While Chris was still enrolled in this school, a friend of Patty's, who had a daughter five years older than Chris, told her about the Avalon School in Orlando, which has been around since 1986 and is run by a lovely family. We enrolled Chris there starting in fifth grade.

Avalon's philosophy is that all minds can learn and succeed and that we all learn differently. Children with Down syndrome are typically very visual learners and do much better when they receive visual aids. Each class had ten or twelve students, and all of the students had some kind of special needs. Chris was the least capable of the students, but they all had a difficult time in a standard school system and found far more success with the individual attention in the smaller classrooms. We were also happy that Chris made a good friend, named Sam, who joined the school at the same time. They became best buddies and are still best friends today.

Families that include kids with Down syndrome have been fighting a frustrating and largely unsuccessful battle for years to get their children mainstreamed into public schools. It is a difficult battle, one that most people do not have the background or resources to wage with any degree of success. Many parents lack the resources to understand the educational and legal issues around inclusion. I am fortunate to have read a lot of books on the subject. Patty and I are just stubborn enough to deal with circumstances when they arise, such as getting Chris into the school when he was in kindergarten. Patty has been willing and able to do the research necessary to learn about new opportunities. This includes new schools, programs, and specialists who are doing innovative things to help parents achieve real breakthroughs with their children.

I have come to believe something that may upset many parents who have experienced frustrations in trying to get their children into a regular school system. It might be counter-intuitive, but it comes from my personal experiences with Chris: perhaps young people with Down syndrome should not aspire for full inclusion within standard educational systems.

Perhaps spending all this time trying to mainstream our children is a mistake—one rooted in love and a desire to do the best we can for them, but a mistake nonetheless. In hindsight, now that we have come to understand how Chris learns, trying to place him in a fully inclusive environment with other kids may not have been the best thing for him.

Some children don't learn particularly well in traditional classroom settings in which the children attend five or six classes every day, moving regularly from one to the next and seamlessly switching gears each time. Children with learning disabilities should not be expected to follow this regimen. Instead, they should focus on one topic at a time and master it through patient repetition, then go on to the next, and so on. They cannot switch gears like other kids and learn five or six things at a time. Patty and I learned that whether it was reading, writing, math, music, or learning to ride a bike, run, or even play golf, we could teach Chris far more quickly using our method of slow, methodical repetition than he would ever learn in any school setting. So instead of taking six classes in a day, kids with Down syndrome would do much better having three classes that are twice as long. I don't know the best way to handle this, but the current system does not work for our children.

Chris spent eight years at Avalon. This is why we can never say enough about the wonderful people at Avalon. Its founder and directors, the Shafers, along with the staff, give so much of themselves to children who are not their own. We will always feel a special bond with the school and the Shafer family.

◆ ◆ ◆

While Patty took charge of Chris's overall care and education, I was involved in developing his interests and abilities in sports. I was like many dads and moms who played sports themselves and couldn't imagine raising a child without introducing lots of opportunities to be physically active. Exercise has many benefits that make us healthier in every conceivable way. Exercise also makes us smarter, more confident, and more independent. All of these things are important for everyone, especially somebody like Chris, who began life with physical and intellectual disabilities. Patty and I looked for every opportunity we could to build athletics into Chris's life.

One of Chris's first exposures to the empowering world of sports came from his babysitter, Leigh. It turned out that Leigh's brother was Hunter Kemper, a triathlete who competed as a US Olympic team member in 2000, 2004, 2008, and 2012, finishing as high as seventh in his third Olympic Games. Chris, Patty, and I used to love hearing her stories of his greatest races in this grueling event that tested the extremes of human endurance.

When Chris was nine years old, we registered him for Special Olympics, which sponsored a series of golf outings at a nearby course. Once a week we took Chris to the course and watched him chip and putt. The Special Olympics version was similar to target golf, with each player getting to take one swing at the ball, trying to get it in the hole. Sometimes they got to take two swings: a chip and a putt. The players received some instruction from the specialists who directed the games. We did this for about three months, and I could tell that Chris had a blast hitting the ball and talking to the specialists and other kids involved with Special Olympics. When the season ended, I thought about continuing with private lessons from one of the players, but Chris wasn't particularly enthusiastic about continuing to play by himself. Still, we were happy to see how much he had enjoyed the game and the social aspect, and I wanted to keep the momentum going.

Eager to find something else for Chris to do, I enrolled him in the Special Olympics track program. Chris did all kinds of events. He ran the hundred- and two-hundred-meter events and threw the shot put. During the basketball season, he played with Special Olympics as well. Special Olympics programs are structured to allow athletes who progress quickly to continue and compete at higher levels in regional and state Special Olympics. Chris did not reach the level where he could compete at these events until he was thirteen. That year he was the only Special Olympian who competed in the shot put. At the state Special Olympics, he threw the shot put alone and uncontested. Everybody cheered his throws, which was the sweetest thing to see. During these years, we were just happy to see Chris having fun and being active. We were not trying to push him to excel at any particular sport because, quite honestly, we didn't think he could.

When you have a child with Down syndrome, you have to think differently. We saw Special Olympics as a means for Chris to be able to play as other kids did—kids who ran around the playgrounds or gyms or ball fields. If he had shown up where other kids played, he would not have been included. Special Olympics filled an important gap. In addition, some small, local basketball and soccer leagues were designed for kids who were not advanced enough to play in the other youth sports programs. Chris played in these leagues as well. Because he loved basketball, we always tried to place him in camps that would accommodate him.

Just as importantly, the people who volunteer to work with kids at Special Olympics and basketball leagues are a very caring, high-caliber group of people. So are the families who take part in Special Olympics. Chris made friends playing different sports. He made friends with other athletes, some of whom had different disabilities. Far fewer kids with Down syndrome compete in Special Olympics than kids with other disabilities, such as autism. Most of the events Chris participated in had ten to twenty times more kids with disabilities other than Down syndrome. The reason for this is obvious: kids with Down syndrome have far greater physical and intellectual disabilities than most other kids, even those who compete in Special Olympics.

Chris started his Special Olympics participation as a decided underdog. The truly inspiring thing about him was win or lose, he was always happy after the race. He could finish dead last but still be ecstatic, walking up to people and high-fiving them and saying, "Nice job," like a good sport. A wound-up guy like me never competed with the kind of heart my son did. I wished I could be a little more like him. I would look at him after a race and think, *With all your disadvantages, how can you be so happy?*

PART 2

6

NEW SETBACKS,
NEW RESOLVE

At some point in 2011, I began to lose feeling in my leg. Over the course of several months, I went in for a bunch of tests, but nobody could figure out what was wrong. And then one day I lost control of my bowel movements, which totally freaked me out.

I called one of my best friends, who was a fraternity brother at Johns Hopkins and is now an orthopedic surgeon. "Hey, Tommy, you're not going to believe this, but . . ." And I told him what happened.

The words "What do you think?" had barely escaped my mouth when my friend said, "Get yourself to a hospital *now!*" When I asked why, he repeated, "Just get yourself to a hospital. I'll arrange to find somebody to meet you there."

One of the best neurosurgeons in town, also a Johns

Hopkins alumnus, met me at the hospital and whisked me up to a room where MRIs were undertaken. (One of the side benefits of going to Johns Hopkins is that you end up knowing a lot of doctors!) I couldn't think of anything that would have caused this kind of injury and chalked it up to an injury I must have had growing up, but couldn't remember, which was compounded through a life spent cramming my body into airplane seats and sitting at a desk. After the examination ended, the doctor came back to read the scans and said, "Hey, Nik, you are lucky you were able to walk in here. I have a surgery this morning, after which I planned to go on vacation. I just postponed it a day because we're going into surgery tonight!"

Three of my vertebrae were collapsing on my spine. If I had twisted my neck the wrong way, there was a possibility that I would have severed my spine. The operation to repair my vertebrae involved separating the collapsing ones from one another and locking them in place with screws. At first the doctor said this would involve two surgeries: one to fix the front of my neck and one to fix the back of my neck. In the end he suggested we go with just one surgery, knowing we might need to come back for a second one later. As the doctor explained this to me, I realized that I was going to be down for a while, so I called my office manager and asked her to come to the hospital and bring anything that needed to be signed. I had surgery that night. A few days later I went home, and my neurosurgeon friend got to go on his vacation. Recovery took six months of inactivity and therapy. Over time I changed my behavior from sitting at work to standing. That actually made a huge difference, something I wish I had done much earlier in my career and would highly recommend to everyone. It's much easier than it sounds, and the value is amazing.

But I didn't regain anything like my former level of physical activity. I would try to get myself motivated, but it would only last for a short time. I'm not the kind of person who puts on a ton of weight from being sedentary. I just become a softer and weaker version of myself, which is not good. The longer I am inactive, the more my muscles atrophy and reapply pressure on my back and neck. I may have looked reasonably fit, but I didn't feel great.

By 2012 I had been devoting myself full-time to growing my sales consulting business, which I called Sales Optimizer. In a typical year we would have contracts with somewhere between twenty to forty companies that would range from a prized million-dollar client to a handful of $400,000 clients and several clients in the $50,000 to $100,000 range. We were enjoying a $5 million revenue run rate, which was very good, but I was easily working close to sixty hours a week for months on end. I chalked it up to the life of an entrepreneur, which involves wearing multiple hats and doing a little bit of everything. First, I designed the programs, then I sold them, and finally I served as a consultant who did billable work that allowed me to make the company more profitable and grow.

The primary product we sell at Sales Optimizer is training for large companies' sales teams. We are a full-blown sales transformation solution that designs a company's entire sales process, which includes software on the Salesforce platform and training people how to use it all. My background in engineering ensured I focused on measurable results in everything I did. When I started the company, I actually called it Focus on Measurable Results before I landed on Sales Optimizer because it better conveyed what we did. That, and it sounded better. I like having an elevator speech in which I can capture what I do by describing myself as a "sales transformation consultant who focuses on results. I measure everything."

I began to apply the concept of 1% Better in my presentations to sales organizations. The concept has many roots, from the *kaizen* way to Eliyahu Goldratt's book *The Goal: A Process of Ongoing Improvement*, and it has been reinforced by the success of the British cycling team and Sir Dave Brailsford's concept of marginal gains. It was also recently made popular by James Clear's bestselling book *Atomic Habits: An Easy and Proven Way to Build Good Habits and Break Bad Ones*. Clear's idea is that those who strive to be in the top 1 percent in whatever they are pursuing need to focus on making many small changes over time rather than one or two major pivots. These small changes most often involve daily habits that increase productivity. The goal is not to overhaul yourself but to improve yourself, much as John Wooden used to espouse, by 1 percent every day.

I'll go over the details in part 3 of this book, but the concepts in all of these bestselling books apply in a measurable, quantitative manner to basic sales metrics. They also have the potential to generate exponential increases in revenues. In other words, building the right habits or practices leads to tiny 1 percent increments, which, over time, generate many multiples of gains—a compounding effect that always had my audiences reaching for their calculators to follow along.

I've always considered myself to be an entrepreneur, but thinking you are one versus actually being one are very different matters. I started my business by getting funding from investors, which enabled me to buy the talent to design the kind of software I needed and bring in a few employees. A few years into the business, I did what many entrepreneurs do and flirted with bankruptcy as my revenues were unable to keep pace with my investments into the company. But I managed to find a way to recover and work my way out of it for the next four or five years, just continuing to slowly build the business. We must have been growing at a better clip than I thought because for four years (2009, 2011, 2012, and 2013) we made the Inc. 5000 list of the fastest-growing companies in America. We weren't Apple, that's for sure, but we built a fairly sophisticated sales operation that saw us through the ups and downs, including my neck surgery.

Raising Chris was a full-time job for Patty, and she excelled at juggling all of the therapists and personal attention he needed. I had a role during those years, especially with keeping Chris active, but those years were all about Patty taking on the responsibilities for giving him the foundation for growing up and fulfilling his potential. In 2016 I decided to become more involved with Chris, but something was going to have to give, and that something proved to be my business.

I was the company's chief salesperson and strategic planner, so it was difficult to have to turn over the company's operations to other people, but it had to be done. I began hiring other people to do some of the consulting, which undercut our ability to grow the business and make enough profit to reinvest in the company. We continued to fulfill our contracts with our clients, but we had to scale back our efforts to pursue new contracts. Not only was I unable to grow the business, but I had to hire and pay more people to carry out the contracts we already had.

When you grow up poor, you have financial insecurities and fears that never quite leave you. These emotions make you especially worried about the absence of money, which in turn leads to becoming relentless in your pursuit to ensure that you have money coming in no matter what. The most stressful part of running a business is worrying about not being able to make payroll and having to tell people who have worked for you for years that they don't have a job.

But I was also influenced enough by my faith to know that regardless of how we plan out our lives to overcome our fears and be strong, God has His own plans for us—and God's plans are better than our own. If our plans, and not God's plans, had prevailed, I would have continued to spend thousands of hours building my business. Patty would have continued spending even more hours nurturing Chris and running our busy household. Chris would have grown up to be a different kind of person than he has become. If our plans, and not God's plans, had prevailed, you would not be reading this book today.

◆ ◆ ◆

When I stepped out of the day-to-day of running my business and stepped deeper into the world of caring for Chris, I let my mind drift more and more to the worldview that prevailed about the lives of people with Down syndrome. I had come to know many families who were raising a child with Down syndrome and understood all of the sacrifices they had to make to give their child a happy home and as healthy a life as they could. I knew they loved their children as we did our own. But I also felt that they—and we—lived with a false narrative about the purpose of life for somebody like Chris. The more I thought about it, the gloomier it seemed.

I thought about how shallow and how empty the life of a person with Down syndrome can be. The highlight of the lives of too many people with Down syndrome—a highlight I have seen reinforced by society—always seems to be that cutesy moment when the now-adult child wins Employee of the Month bagging groceries at the local store. Most of these people pretty much dropped off the face of the earth at the age of eighteen because they were done with school while all their classmates went on to college. At this point they lived lives of relative seclusion and isolation from the community. I could see this happening to Chris despite all that Patty and I had done to care and provide for him.

I realized we needed to do something different. We needed to see whether Chris could do more and live a better life—one that didn't end in a cute moment at eighteen but stretched on into adulthood where he might do something that was substantive, something that would benefit him for the rest of his life and benefit others like him.

From the moment Chris was born, we were told about all of the things he would not be able to do. We were warned about setting high expectations for him—about setting any kind of expectations, to be honest—because we would just be inviting disappointment. The obstacles were too high, and we would probably end up hurting him if we pushed him too hard and set high goals for him.

We needed to be *realistic.*

Realistic. Really?

How could we know what Chris was capable of without giving him a chance to *show* what he was capable of? The most basic lesson of learning how to succeed is learning how to fail first, right? Why shouldn't we have given him a chance to find his way out of failure and into success like the rest of us? It was time to stop being *realistic* and to shift into a higher gear. We needed to take the lid off. We had to be adventurous with Chris. *We had to take risks.* After all, I reasoned, my parents were not being realistic when they resolved to leave a dead-end existence in Yugoslavia and risk everything by fleeing to America. And being realistic wasn't going to help Chris find a meaningful place in my adopted country. Being realistic, I thought, was highly overrated.

The problem with accepting being realistic is that it leads nowhere. When Chris was three or four, all the other kids would go into preschool and kindergarten and leave him behind. Nobody would make room for Chris because they thought he couldn't handle it mentally or physically. As I mentioned earlier, between kindergarten and sixth grade, we moved him around to eight different schools because, one way or another, somebody did not want to work with him. Maybe it was a teacher, a principal, or even his classmates. You can try to force them to accept your child, which we did on one occasion, but gradually all the fighting wears you down, and you lose hope because it seems nobody can think outside the box.

Let me tell you something important about Chris, something that might explain a little bit about this journey we are on and the hard line I have felt I needed to take to set up a new set of expectations for him—expectations that traditional institutions could not or would not make. Chris is an incredible romantic and has been since he was a small child. As soon as he could talk at eight or nine years old, he wanted to get married, preferably to a blond woman who looked like his mom. He also wanted to have a house and a car. When Jacky was a teenager, she had a DVD collection of *Friends*. Chris used to watch *Friends* and hit Pause every time Rachel, played by Jennifer Aniston, came on the screen. Jacky would go to watch a program and see smooch marks on the screen where Chris had laid a little kiss on Rachel. It was innocent, of course, but Patty ruled that there would be no watching *Friends* anymore while Chris was awake!

And it was not as though he just loved beautiful women; he also built up this whole notion of what romance was all about. Once when Jacky was home from college for the summer, she took Chris out for ice cream. This would have been when Chris was eleven or twelve and Jacky was a college senior. When they returned, she could barely stop laughing as she tried to tell me about her conversation with Chris on the ride over. Apparently he had seen an advertisement on television for a couples' getaway at some exotic location such as Bora Bora. It was some kind of package deal that included flowers in the room, champagne toasts, quiet dinners under the cabana, daily massages, and moonlight walks on the beach. I am fairly sure Chris did not know what champagne was, but he began asking Jacky whether she planned to go out and have a romantic dinner with wine and champagne. Jacky doesn't drink and tried to explain to Chris that you don't need wine to have a romantic evening, but Chris was having none of it.

"You need to have wine for it to be romantic," he kept saying.

Chris has always been highly attuned to those types of things. He often begins sentences by saying, "One day when I have a wife and we're married, we'll . . ." We are convinced that his deepest desire is to find a woman whom he will love more than anything and who will love and adore him in return. And together they will do all sorts of things and see the world. All of us dream of a future, however vague, that we hope we can have. Many of us include somebody we fall in love with as part of this dream. Chris has felt these yearnings more powerfully than most people I have known. To this day he dreams of having a house and a wife and being a part of a community.

Even groups that existed solely to help seemed incapable of imagining any alternative future for someone like Chris. Organizations such as the Down Syndrome Association can provide a community of people going through the same things as you. I became intensely involved with the group soon after Chris was born and even became a part of the association's board. Yet even with this resource at our disposal, we were not learning or hearing anything offering us much hope or direction for acting any way other than *realistically*. Maybe it was my business mindset, but I began to think about the ways that risk-taking and relying on trial and error, the same things I used to come up with innovative ways of teaching sales technique, might apply to helping Chris.

In 2016 Chris and I started doing a little biking and light running together. We also swam together, and Chris continued to compete in the local Special Olympics. We both enjoyed the sunshine, and working out brought us together for father-son time, which Chris always loved. We actually started doing short triathlons as a way to get in shape. Chris also liked exercising for another reason: it meant that a snack was waiting for him when the exercise ended, and one thing Chris loves almost as much as a hug is a bowl of ice cream with his favorite topping and a good TV show. It was during this time, however, that I realized I was going to have to undergo more surgeries on my shoulder and one on my hip. (I'd like to go on record right here and say anybody who denies that getting older sucks isn't being honest.)

On top of this, Chris began to have problems with his ears, which signaled the beginning of a period when Chris would need to have multiple ear surgeries. The compressed facial features of people with Down syndrome often disrupt their nasal passages and lead to ear infections. Typical babies and toddlers face these issues as well, but they usually outgrow them. Chris did not and eventually had to have surgeries to clean out the growth, reconstruct his ear canals, and open them up. He had to undergo four such surgeries on his ears during a two-year period from 2016 through the end of 2017.

The ear surgeries took a serious toll on Chris's fitness and attitude. By the time the last surgery was completed and he healed in the early months of 2018, Chris had been sedentary for close to two years, with each surgery requiring about six months of recovery time. One day I walked into our family room and found Chris sitting on the sofa playing a video game. I sat down and looked over at him and just thought about the two of us. There we were, both of us recovering from surgeries and neither of us presenting our best version of ourselves. Chris wasn't thinking along these lines, but I sure was.

The doctors who performed Chris's surgeries had strongly advised that we keep Chris as far away from the water as possible because, they said, the water pressure would be bad for him. I did not take this news very well. In fact, I didn't take it at all. Before the surgeries, Chris had been on a roll with the exercises he and I were doing, and the last thing I wanted to do was throw up another long blockade for him to jump over on the way to recovery. So we got a little creative and decided that when he was swimming, he would wear ear plugs to prevent water from getting in. If you ever see a photograph of Chris competing, you'll notice he wears a tight-fitting cap. The cap is there to hold the ear plugs snugly in place. That was the end of the problem as far as we were concerned.

I was still convinced that the key to giving Chris a better life involved him becoming more physically active and involved in the community. Whatever dreams and aspirations Chris had, whatever God had in store for him, our son would never live up to his potential if he spent his life sitting on a couch playing video games. The video games might be a well-earned reward for applying himself in other ways, such as becoming physically active and involved in the community, but the time had come to refocus his body and his mind. It was time to stop being realistic and start shaking things up. We had to stop settling for too little out of life. Our son deserved more—and it was time for me to challenge him and expand his horizons.

I could play a major part in helping him grow and fulfill his potential. Chris was starting to tease me by telling me that I was old and weak and frail whenever he saw me limping around the house or groaning while getting up from the couch. And that would never do. He was right: years of working too much and sitting too much had destroyed my body and turned me into an old man. I began thinking about how to get both of us back up and on the road again.

7

LET'S DO ONE MORE

When Chris and I resumed our exercise routine in 2018, I was doing a fair amount of reading about the athletic potential of people with Down syndrome and discovered videos of a gymnast named Chelsea Werner. She was a four-time champion in the US Special Olympics and a two-time Special Olympics World Champion who went on to have a modeling career. I watched a video of her doing pull-ups and sit-ups and flips on the bars and thought, *Holy jeepers!* Here was somebody who could do things that 99 percent of the population, disabled or not, cannot do. Chelsea's achievements made her look confident and empowered instead of just cute. These videos of Chelsea gave me exactly what I had been looking for: an example of what people like Chris can do when they are given the gift of having higher expectations placed on them.

No sooner had I begun to think along these lines than a woman named Victoria Johnson from the Special Olympics Florida office called us and asked if Chris would be interested in joining a new pilot program for triathletes. "We're trying to see if we can find athletes who can do a triathlon," said Victoria. "We know it's a stretch, but we think our athletes can do it. What do you think?" I thought for one-tenth of a nanosecond and answered yes. Special Olympics had put out a call and managed to sign up a handful of athletes—including my son. It was time to push him off the couch and away from the video games, and now he would have a concrete program to provide structure to his exercise.

I remember breaking the news to my family one evening when Jacky was visiting us. She had already graduated from Dartmouth, where she studied economics and digital design and played basketball, and had returned to Florida. Now a certified personal trainer, she was running her own business as a fitness and nutrition coach while also working with me as a sales coach at Sales Optimizer. Jacky will be the first one to tell you that she is in the business of helping people get the bodies they want so they feel better—and that focusing on strength training, developing muscle tone, and adopting healthy eating habits are the surest route to meeting these goals.

"Cardio just ruins your body," Jacky told me. "Don't get him into *that*! Get him into powerlifting or something along those lines."

I knew that Jacky believed in Chris's potential to do great things as much as I did. She always told people, "My brother has a disability. He's not disabled." She knew from playing dominoes with Chris that her little brother had the same competitive spirit she had. But even more important to Jacky's way of thinking, Chris had something special to give the world. He radiated love and joy that were meant to be shared beyond our immediate family. "Something is going to happen at some point," she'd promise. "I don't know when or what it will be, but something is going to happen."

And I knew that while Patty always wanted to protect Chris, she also wanted him to be happy. So this time around, I decided to take a more businesslike approach by setting goals with Chris, taking the 1% Better concept I used in sales training and applying it to his athletic training.

Muhammad Ali once joked that he didn't start counting sit-ups until it hurt. Chris wasn't Muhammad Ali, so I decided to measure and record his progress from the start. I also thought about the powerful impact John Wooden had made on me all those years ago. How would Coach Wooden approach training for a triathlon? Well, he certainly wouldn't begin by fixating on the final product. Coach Wooden would focus on the process of becoming a better athlete. He would focus on developing good habits as the building blocks for progress over time. He wouldn't rush things, but he wouldn't waste time either. The one constant would be gradual change—something that the 1% Better concept recognizes and embraces.

When Chris resumed his training, I tried to explain the 1% Better concept to him, but he couldn't grasp it. So I talked to him in a way that kept his focus on getting a little bit better each day. "Hey, buddy," I'd say, "we're going to have fun and do a little bit better each day and see how well we can do." Chris was all on board with that. So on the first day we biked for a mile. The next day we went a little farther, maybe another mile or maybe just another half mile. The next day we might have done a lap in the pool and followed that up with an additional lap the next time we swam. Each time we did something, we always did one more. "One more" became our little mantra in those early months of getting in shape.

For example, when Chris worked on strengthening his core with push-ups, sit-ups, and squats, he started with one of each. Then a second set of one, and eventually he got to four sets of fifty. If he did four sets of forty on Monday, then on Tuesday I would say, "Chris, do your 1 percent more today." He knew he needed to do four sets of forty-one. Adding one more made the additional exercise very manageable for Chris since he would have a day or two to rest in between. If Chris rode ten sets of ten loops around the neighborhood on his bike on a Saturday, then the next Saturday he would do ten sets of eleven loops.

There are four levels of officially recognized triathlons. Beginners just entering the triathlon scene typically start competing in what are called "sprints." Sprint triathlons include swimming half a mile, cycling 12.4 miles, and running 3.1 miles. A sprint triathlon is a perfect entry-level event, but it also offers a sufficient challenge for athletes of all levels looking to fine-tune their bodies and gain more race experience. Olympic triathlons face a 0.93-mile swim, a 24.8-mile bike ride, and a 6.2-mile run, exactly double the length of a sprint triathlon. From there, very ambitious athletes can attempt to take on an IRONMAN 70.3 triathlon, which includes a 1.2-mile swim, 56 miles of cycling, and a 13.1-mile run. And the most ambitious athletes can go for the IRONMAN triathlon, which is a full distance race totaling 140.6 miles.

Over the course of several months, I continued to measure Chris's progress a little bit at a time when we trained. I also tracked his improvement from one event to the next. He did his first sprint triathlon in 148 minutes, and three sprint events later, he finished in 100 minutes. When I did the math, I found, low and behold, he was improving at a clip of about 1 percent each day.

But Chris wasn't just improving—he was having an absolute blast. Like his mother, Chris is a very social person, so the presence of hundreds of people at the Clearwater sprint was exciting for him. When we went to register for the race, we noticed a tent where people could go after the race was over to get a massage. Chris saw a blond woman preparing the massage tables and went up to her to ask what she was doing. She told him she was getting ready to give massages to the participants after they finished their races. Now, we were visiting her before the race, but Chris didn't seem to care and asked her if he could have a quick massage. She said, "Sure," and gave him one. Needless to say, he stopped by after the race for another one.

Chris loves the energy around any kind of athletic event. He also likes the attention he receives as one of the athletes. In 2019 Chris ran in six sprints, four Special Olympics events and two that were sponsored by a local triathlon club. Triathlons are difficult events for any organization to put on. They require access to a lake and someplace where you can have a bike course and a running course. The organizers often have to close roads to traffic, which requires hiring a police officer to monitor intersections. There are also insurance matters. To increase the number of events offered to athletes, Special Olympics sometimes partners with local clubs that run the events. The clubs give Special Olympics athletes their own division in the race. Other than that, the races are identical, with the same distances and time limits.

In August 2019 Chris ran a 16-mile sprint triathlon at a Special Olympics event in Florida. He said he was feeling a little off that day, a little sluggish. His time of 1 hour and 41 minutes earned him last place among Special Olympics athletes competing that day and last among all participants. Since our goal was to run and be healthy and independent, not to bring home lots of trophies, Chris was proud to finish the race. While Chris is generally a happy person, win or lose, he is also a proud young man who doesn't actually *enjoy* finishing last, especially when he had a girlfriend who was a gymnast and was chosen to compete at the Special Olympics World Games in Abu Dhabi. He was finishing last, and she was punching her ticket. I felt his pain, so we began to think more about the long term.

Maybe we could work hard for a couple of years with the goal of competing in the 2022 Special Olympics USA Games, which were scheduled to take place in Orlando. If he did well enough there by placing in the top three, perhaps he would get the chance to go to Germany in 2023 to compete in the Berlin World Games. That's how inspiration can start sometimes. You see other people around you achieving wonders and getting lots of well-earned attention, and you get a little inspired. You say to yourself, *I want some of that too! If I outwork everybody else like I think I can, why should I watch from the sidelines while they get all the attention?*

Chris and I started talking about getting deeper into triathlons as a route to Special Olympics USA and then the World Games. Between August and October we picked up the pace and rigor of his training. In October he joined hundreds of other people to swim one thousand meters in open water at a lake near where we live. This distance exceeded that of an Olympic-level sprint. It was not a competitive race, but every week people show up and swim together across the lake. The guy who sponsors the swim owns a house that is more or less on the shoreline where the swimmers finish. In accordance with tradition, the first time people swim across and back, they are welcome to sign their names on the wall of the owner's house.

I honestly think that our conversations about the World Games flashed through his mind after he completed the swim across the lake because he signed his name "Chris World Champion." He might literally have meant world champion, but he also might have meant, "Chris Nikic, amazing dude who is fulfilling his dreams!"

After his big swim across the lake, it was time for Chris to take on something a little bigger. I was tracking all his workouts and noticed that he continued to improve an average of 1 percent per day on just about everything from push-ups to his bike rides, swims, and runs. He was improving so fast that I began to wonder just how much he was capable of achieving. We made the decision to spend November and December getting him ready to attempt his first Olympic triathlon in Sarasota, Florida. The event was held January 6, 2020. In the space of only three months, he would go from racing 16 miles to 32 miles. That meant we had roughly sixty days to get Chris ready for a race that was more than twice as long as the one he was used to. Triathletes will tell you that as you go from one distance to the next, the degree of difficulty is not 100 percent but more like 300 percent to 500 percent. So going from a sprint to an Olympic is not twice as hard but several times as hard. The same is true going from an Olympic to an IRONMAN 70.3 triathlon and on to a full distance. It makes sense: When you do a sprint, you start fresh and are exhausted when you complete the race. When you do an Olympic, after you have finished a sprint, you are exhausted but must do *another* sprint!

We were fortunate at this point to add another member to Chris's team—Dan Grieb. Dan had a successful real estate team in Florida and was a veteran triathlete and IRONMAN triathlon competitor. Having made his fortune in business, he was looking for a meaningful volunteer project and, long story short, discovered Chris. Dan ran with Chris during the January triathlon, and the two of them have been training together ever since.

Chris and Dan finished the Olympic triathlon in four and a half hours. This was the moment when everything began to change at a faster clip, and we took the ceiling off our thinking. One of his best friends, Abigail, who was born six days apart from Chris and also has Down syndrome, posted her congratulations on Facebook. That post got something like seventeen thousand views. It was just as Jacky had predicted: Chris was beginning to assert himself on a larger stage.

As Chris prepared to do an Olympic triathlon, another

big shift took place in my personal thinking. I started to compare how I viewed and treated Chris to how I viewed and treated Jacky. You see, I viewed Jacky as gifted, so I treated her like that. I invested significant amounts of time coaching Jacky to realize her gifts, and she did just that. But I viewed and treated Chris as special, so I protected him. At that point I realized I was both the problem and the solution. So I decided that from then on I was going to view and treat Chris as gifted, same as Jacky. Oh man, did his and my world change when I replaced just one word in our vocabulary!

At that point, at least in my own mind, we were going to go for an IRONMAN triathlon. I thought, *I'm going to take Chris on a mental and physical journey and see how far we can go. I see something in him that nobody else is quite seeing. I want to give him a chance without anybody planting a negative seed in him.*

One of the things the 1% Better method teaches is that you need to control the controllable. If I wanted to help Chris maximize his potential, I had to help establish habits that would improve not only his training but also his diet, sleep, and mental fortitude, and I had to monitor his progress. This meant, to a larger degree than I would have imagined, limiting peoples' access to him and ensuring that those who had anything to do with him—including his own family—spoke to him in a positive way. I wasn't worried that people would say hurtful or mean-spirited things to him. I thought that people might infer to Chris that something within his grasp was out of reach. I had been hearing about things being out of reach for too long. It was time to cut that out, especially when Chris was thriving.

Of course, I was not running a small dictatorship. Chris and I are always going back and forth. We negotiate just about everything together. I regularly asked his opinion on things, and he regularly asked for mine. Being his father, I often share my opinions regardless of whether he asks for them. But that's my job, and it goes beyond being a parent! I have spent thirty years working as a corporate coach. I am used to working closely with people and communicating honestly with them. I cannot imagine where he gets it from, but Chris is very opinionated and strong-willed. He definitely has his own ideas. But I have found that he is also a terrific student who is willing to be coached and admit that I offer a certain wisdom and knowledge born of years of experience. In fact, I credit much of Chris's success to him being the most coachable person I have ever coached in my life.

Chris told me he wanted to be a world champ at something, so on New Year's Eve 2019, I asked Chris to write down his dreams. He wrote down that he wanted to buy his own car, buy his own house, and marry a wonderful woman like his mom. After he wrote out his dreams, I said to Chris that if he sat on the couch all day watching TV and playing video games, he would never get his dreams. If he did an IRONMAN triathlon and became a motivational speaker, he had a chance to achieve his dreams. He was going to have to keep those dreams front and center in his mind, especially when the training got tough.

When I told Patty and Jacky about my plan to prepare Chris for an IRONMAN race, they responded predictably. Patty was clearly uncomfortable with the idea. Jacky upped the ante by asking me whether I was "freakin' crazy." When

I told them that the race we planned to do was only eleven months away, Patty furrowed her brow, and Jacky gave me one of her "what the . . . ?" looks.

"A well-conditioned athlete would need longer than eleven months to train for a full distance IRONMAN race," Jacky protested. "And you want Chris to do it? You are crazy!"

Oh, we were very serious, I assured her.

Chris was helped by a small circle of people who love and trust each other. We pushed what was possible, and our life stories are blended together in a way that holds a certain magic. By helping Chris achieve his dreams, by continuing to push for continuous improvement—even if it was only by 1 percent a day—our experience provides a model other people can follow as they look to improve their lives, their work, and their efforts. I guess I'm putting that engineering degree to use after all.

8

TEAM CHRIS

I love to coach, and I think I am a good coach, especially when it comes to my own child's development. I also keenly felt the need to step up as a father and be around for Chris as much as possible—certainly more than I had during his childhood. But Chris needed somebody to spend a lot more time with him than I could give, especially since I had a business to run. IRONMAN triathlon competitions and the necessary training are so intense, we had to put our trust in a larger team. Each member of Chris's team had a different relationship with him. Each of them contributed different skills and experiences, though our roles sometimes overlapped. Training for an IRONMAN event, even one scheduled eleven months later, would challenge the physical and mental resources of the greatest athletes. Training for a young man with Down syndrome truly took a team.

To keep Chris on track and balance our various schedules, we chose Sunday evenings to meet up on the phone to assess the previous week and plan for the coming one. Some of our meetings grew heated, but in the end our shared love for Chris produced a collaboration I am still proud of to this day. The truth is sometimes we have to remind ourselves that what brings our team together every day is Chris. We are all passionate people who have been successful in our careers. Most of us are type A personalities, and that ensures we are driven in everything we do. Sometimes this has created some acrimony in our relationships. I'll get to that after introducing Team Chris.

I am the head coach. Even the most devoted and caring volunteers in the world, like the ones on our team, cannot devote the energy and passion that a parent can. I watched Chris's overall mental and physical development and charted his progress. I was also honest with Chris about steadily improving. I am blessed to have Chris's implicit trust. Our bond is so strong that even when everyone else has failed to raise his spirits, I can say a few words, and he will immediately push through the barriers. I have done this when he is down on himself. I have quieted his fears after a bad fall. I have kept him going even when the pain of pushing forward grows unbearable. I don't tell Chris what to do or how to feel. I remind him of his dreams and ask him if he is willing to keep going to get them.

As Chris's head coach, I set the overall strategy, which involved having Chris get into the habit of making incremental daily improvements and weekly gains. My primary objective in all of this was to build his mind. I believe success starts and ends in the mind, and if you build the mind, the body will follow. At first there was very little progress and activity. Over time, as making an effort became more of a habit, Chris's activity increased, and he made major improvements in his training workload and finish times in the triathlons. Identifying what Chris really wanted and using it to motivate him was important. We used food and his dream of getting married and buying a house to motivate him to focus on daily improvements. I don't believe for one second that Chris's main goal was to complete an IRONMAN triathlon as an end in itself. I'm not even sure just how much he understands the benefits of exercise to his health and mental acuity. But I know for certain that he wanted to belong, to feel valued and needed. And if finishing an IRONMAN triathlon advanced that goal, he was going to go all in.

As part of the Special Olympics triathlon pilot, Chris had been assigned a guide named Simone Goodfriend. Simone describes herself as a so-so athlete but a passionate volunteer who joined Special Olympics as a swim coach out of her deep-seated belief that it was her duty to give back to her community. I think she's understating her athlete talents but not her passion to help.

Special Olympics staff includes coaches who design and lead training sessions and programs. The staff also includes "Unified partners," athletes without disabilities who participate with Special Olympics athletes during formal training sessions and in the events. All Special Olympics athletes must have a Unified partner to participate. Simone started as Chris's Unified partner.

Simone and Chris first met in 2018, during the big kickoff

meeting when Special Olympics staff explained how the tri-athlon worked and set up some initial training sessions. Chris and Simone took to each other at once.

Before Simone arrived on the scene, I served as Chris's Unified partner. In March 2018 Chris and I decided to get our feet wet by doing a 5-mile triathlon sponsored by a local club in Clearwater, Florida. I think the course included a 200-meter swim, a mile run, and a 4-mile bike ride. We took part in it to build some fun into our training but also to establish a baseline for measuring our progress. After this event we were scheduled to do another one, but I hurt my back and couldn't make it. I asked Special Olympics if someone else could stand in as Chris's Unified partner. Simone did, and so began a deeper relationship between them.

Most athletes and Unified partners meet only during Special Olympic training and events. When Chris and Simone found out they lived close to each other, they began training together several times a week. Simone had a full-time job, so the two of them would meet after work and on weekends to bike, run, swim, or do strength exercises. The two of them developed a genuine friendship, which involved a lot of laugh-ing and joking around. The Nikic family culture includes a lot of needling and teasing of one another, and Chris had always proved no exception to this. Simone quickly picked up on this trait, and the two of them were constantly trash talking each other in training and in races. At first some of the other Special Olympics personnel were put off by hearing one of their Unified partners telling her athlete with Down syndrome that she was going to kick his ass and leave him so far behind he would need a telescope to see her. "Why are you always behind me?" she would say, egging him on. "Are you trying to look at my butt?" But their concern ended as soon as they heard Chris shoot back that he was faster than her butt any day and was going to whip her so badly she wouldn't know what county she was in.

Despite all the constant joking around and silliness, they never lost sight of what we were trying to accomplish. When Simone started to pull ahead of Chris and said, "Okay, I'll see you, dude. I'm just gonna finish this circuit and see you at the finish line," she was doing more than keeping things fun. She was also motivating him and challenging him to do more. If left to his own devices, Chris would usually try to slow things down and take the easiest path to his goal. But Simone had the touch, and Chris invariably responded to her gibes with a laugh and then would run faster to catch up with her. That was one way he kept pushing and improving.

Since I didn't know anything about triathlons, the second role on the team was to design a workout plan, and that role was filled by Hector Torres. Hector is the head coach of the Central Florida Tri Club and a highly sought-after private coach who has completed twenty-nine IRONMAN triathlons as of this writing. He also served as the head coach of the 2012 USA Paratriathlon Team and has years of experience working with athletes of all levels. In 2018 Special Olympics approached him to design and coach the triathlon pilot in which Chris participated. It was Hector's training sessions that guided Simone and me in the early stages of working with Chris. As Chris progressed from competing in sprints to triathlons, Hector established a training regimen that, if we followed it, would prepare Chris to undertake an IRONMAN triathlon.

Of course, there were no guarantees. There are very few IRONMAN events where everybody finishes under the deadline—or even finishes at all. But Hector's method was tried and proven to work—with a caveat, however: his methods worked for elite athletes and people with above-average mental toughness and motivation. Chris was neither of those.

Hector showed his great respect for Chris by assigning him the same workload he assigned every athlete. But the workload proved to be a key trouble spot in our Sunday evening meetings. The truth was, Chris required a different approach to both workload and environment. For example, one of the training regimens Hector suggested—which was totally state of the art for typical athletes—involved intensive training on a stationary bike indoors. The purpose of this training was to build leg strength in a controlled, efficient way. Hector was drawing on established methods for IRONMAN triathlon training and was frustrated when I said no, this would never do for Chris.

Why, he wanted to know? So I told him that building leg strength was less important for Chris than building his mind by learning how to ride a bicycle outside. It took Chris six months to learn to balance a bike, and he needed to keep training his muscles and his mind to do so. We had to make some adjustments to Hector's proposed sessions because we didn't think Chris could progress as rapidly as the type of triathletes Hector was used to working with. For example, a typical person training for an IRONMAN triathlon would do a six-hour bicycle ride at eighteen or nineteen miles an hour.

Chris could rarely exceed fifteen miles an hour on a bike, so his training sessions required eight hours of riding.

But even more than this, Chris needed to have unlimited opportunities to grow more comfortable with the outdoors. He needed to learn to ride a bike with cars coming around the corner, squirrels darting across the road in front of him, and parents yelling at their kids to come home. He needed to let the sights and sounds of the busy world seep into his subconscious over and over again until things didn't startle him and he could feel comfortable going a little faster and farther each time he trained. In a nutshell, Hector's plan was focused on building the body, and my plan was focused on building Chris's mind first, then his body.

Nobody on Chris's team could deny that this method was working. Chris went from barely riding a bike to riding ten miles with Simone, and he went from pedaling at around eight miles an hour to twelve miles an hour and then fifteen, twenty, and even twenty-five miles an hour. Eventually he was able to maintain a pace over many miles that few others could do—Down syndrome or not! At the point where he was regularly bicycling at twenty miles per hour, I thought, *Whoa, wait a minute. I didn't see this coming.* And then I saw the same compounding effect I had seen in sales. A slow start gradually builds a habit of steady improvement that snowballs the longer you stick with the program, which helps in avoiding the temptation to try to improve too much too quickly and burn out.

Safety is important for anybody taking part in a sport that involves high speeds on a bicycle and road racing. Chris especially needed somebody to be with him during training and events. Our neighborhood offered Chris a fairly private and safe place to train, but even here things could go wrong. As Chris got to a point where he was doing really well and feeling much more comfortable on the bike, his speed started to pick up. One time I was sitting in a lawn chair in the front yard waiting for Chris to come around for another lap, and I looked up just in time to see him pitch forward over the handlebars of his bike and take a very nasty fall when he rounded the last corner. He was so badly banged up that we had to take him to the emergency room for stitches.

Worst of all, this accident spooked him. It took a couple of weeks before we could get him back on a bike and he would push himself again. When we had our next triathlon sprint, for example, he was going so slow that there were runners who had already finished the bike event and were doing the run course, running past Simone and Chris, who were doing about six miles an hour. Simone did everything she could to try to get his mind off his fears, but nothing worked. I was waiting for them close to the finish line and wondered what could be taking them so long. Eventually it became obvious to me that something was wrong, so I started walking the course in reverse and looking for them. When Chris finally saw me, he started crying—out of frustration and disappointment and wanting to please me.

I gave him a hug and reassured him that it was okay to go faster—that the best way not to feel afraid was to push himself to go a little faster again. I reminded him that Simone would be right there to watch over him. Somehow he and Simone finished the race. When the routine you are used to in training is changed and you are facing actual race conditions, stress can be overwhelming. Suddenly lots more people are around you and probably cars, too, during the cycling course. Unfamiliar surroundings can overstimulate and then exhaust someone like Chris. Simone didn't want Chris to associate race events with stress and uncertainty. She wanted him to have fun and fall in love with the actual exercise, so she became proficient at gauging his mood during races. When he seemed worried about people coming too close to him or about falling off the bike or a dog barking and moving toward them, she would exhort him not to worry. "We're not worried about other people or where we finish," she would say to him. "We're just having fun and getting fitter."

Ironically, Hector believed I was pushing Chris too hard at times and told me as much. Hector broke down every workout based on Chris's heart rate, his cadence, and how he was evolving as an athlete, so Hector was in a good position to argue the point. For the most part, I listened and backed off a bit with Chris. I respected Hector's use of metrics because it aligned with my way of thinking. Where we differed was in the approach we took. As I've mentioned, I was adamant about building Chris's mind while Hector was focused on Chris's body. I will explain in more detail later, but this is at the heart of the difference between the 1% Better method and the traditional training methods used by coaches, such as Hector, who coach elite athletes. Their system and approach are designed to maximize performance in the shortest amount of time while the 1% Better method is designed to build the mind and lifelong habits of success. Our method, by its nature, is designed to eliminate the risk of injuries, an attribute that allowed Chris to remain injury-free in the short eleven months leading up to the IRONMAN race.

By the later part of 2019, Chris and Simone had participated in six sprint triathlons, and by August 2019, at the Special Olympics state championships, Chris left Simone in the dust during the bike portion and finished the race on his own, which is a no-no in Special Olympics. The guide is there to guide and protect the athlete, and Simone could not keep up. He had overcome his fears of the bike and the hills. When we decided to tackle an Olympic distance, we needed another guide. An Olympic triathlon was going to be held in January 2020 in Sarasota, Florida, and we targeted that one for Chris. Simone is a strong swimmer and decent runner, but she was losing ground exponentially to Chris when it came to cycling. This was not a minor detail if Chris was going to compete in an Olympic triathlon cycling distance. The bicycling distance in an Olympic triathlon is nearly 25 miles, far too long a distance for Chris to be barreling down the road by himself with cars and other cyclists only a few feet from him.

It was at this time that Dan Grieb came into the picture. Aside from me, Dan would spend more time than anybody with Chris through long runs and swims and even longer bike rides. His own life story made him an especially devoted ally for Chris.

Dan had a difficult childhood, and it was drummed into his head that he would never amount to anything in life. A weaker person might have taken such relentless negativity to heart and let it place severe limitations on him. But Dan is an incredibly strong person with a passion for protecting people who cannot protect themselves. When he was a kid, he took on bullies on behalf of smaller kids, and he dreamed of becoming a police officer. After graduating from the police academy, he took a job in a small police department in Florida. Dan soon discovered that policing was not what he thought it would be, so he looked for another line of work. He found it in Florida real estate, a boom industry into which Dan poured his endless energy. He succeeded in building a highly successful business, but he did so at the cost of his health. At one point during the years in which he built his agency, he grew to three hundred pounds, far too much weight to support on his five-foot-ten frame.

Dan began his own weight-loss journey by doing what Dan does best: going all out. A natural athlete who once dreamed of playing college football, Dan began competing in various types of races, amassing a portfolio of more than one hundred races, including five IRONMAN triathlons and ten IRONMAN 70.3 triathlons. In the process, he lost more than one hundred pounds and discovered a new passion to pour himself into: giving back. That was ultimately what brought him to us.

Dan joined Team Chris as Chris's new Unified partner in late 2019 and was by Chris's side for the 2020 Olympic triathlon Chris completed in January. Their time was 4 hours and 25 minutes to complete the nearly 32 miles of swimming, biking, and running. Not too shabby!

One of the first things Dan had to learn in working with Chris was that the journey had to include the prospect of failure. Dan is a very driven guy who wants to succeed at anything he does, which he usually manages to do, and that included being right beside Chris as he crossed the finish line at the November 2020 IRONMAN triathlon. Dan is an IRONMAN Certified Coach, Certified Performance Coach, and Neuro Linguistic Programming Master Practitioner. Dan's coaching style is intense but with a focus on developing relationships.

As Chris's Unified partner and guide, Dan used to be anxious at the thought that my son might not complete a race. How could Dan live with himself if Chris failed? I helped Dan deal with his fears by asking him a couple of important questions: First, I asked, "Dan, when do you learn life's greatest lessons—when you succeed or when you fail?"

He said, "When you fail."

Then I asked, "Can you give my son the same opportunity to learn though failure?" Dan answered that he would welcome that approach with all his heart.

Since that conversation, Dan has told me how incredibly liberating it was for him to receive my permission to fail with Chris. He was freed from the mindset that leads many coaches to make the mistake of trying to protect their athletes from disappointment. As a coach, Dan has learned that the processing speed of athletes like Chris is a little slower. Dan has to be sure he explains himself fully, including breaking things down into bite-size pieces. He knows he has to push Chris at the proper level. Other than that, competitors like Chris don't want, or even need, to be treated differently. As a Unified partner and guide, Dan is never more than an arm's length away from Chris. While Chris swims well in open water, when they swim in the ocean together, they wear a tether.

Dan and Chris spend a lot of time together, especially during the longer sessions. They usually meet twice a week.

One of Dan's challenges with Chris is keeping him focused. This is easier to do with his strength training and shorter workouts, but as the distances increase, Dan needs more tools to use with Chris. (This would also be true if Dan was coaching you and me.) It's one thing for Dan to say "Just one more lap" when one more means a mile around the neighborhood. It's quite another for him to say "one more" when he is talking about 13 miles. To keep Chris focused and energized, Dan has him count cones that have been spaced out over the long ride. Or they talk about the kind of woman Chris hopes to find and marry someday.

During one of their rides, Chris hit a big bump on his bike and yelled, "Bullshit!"

Dan couldn't believe his ears. "What did you say?"

"Bullshit!" Chris repeated. So the two of them spent the next 10 miles saying, "You're bullshit" and "No, you're bullshit" back and forth to each other. Anything to keep their minds off of what was happening at the time and the pain Chris was in.

◆ ◆ ◆

One of the consolations of training for extreme endurance sports is finding others to share in your pain. During a typical week, Simone would help out with some of Chris's workouts, especially swimming. I was always there, following along in my e-bike either on his bike rides or runs and making sure he had support and proper nutrition. Chris would do about fifteen to twenty workouts per week, an average of two to three times per day. Dan and Simone would join him for several of those workouts, with Dan gradually spending more time with him as the IRONMAN events drew closer.

On weekends Chris had even more companions in misery for his longer training sessions. Hector and Dan are both members of the Central Florida Tri Club. Once we established our goal of doing an IRONMAN triathlon, the word quickly spread around the club that Dan and Chris would welcome any and all club members to join them for their long Saturday ride and Sunday run.

The Tri Club certainly came out in full force for Chris, ensuring that he would never want for a training partner during the long hours of training. Club members Jennifer and Carlos became fixtures in our long weekend workouts. By the time we got into our intense IRONMAN training, Dan, Jennifer, and Carlos were the three who were always there with Chris and me. Eventually this was the team that guided Chris through the IRONMAN race. Dan did the entire event, but Carlos helped with the swim and the run, and Jennifer assisted with the bike and the run. At least two guides were with Chris throughout the race. This was the core Team Chris.

On Saturdays the Tri Club members would get up at four o'clock and bike for more than 50 miles while Chris and I would start our own ride in the safety of our neighborhood. Then some of them would drive over to our house and do the last 50 miles with Chris around our neighborhood after the battery on my e-bike was drained. Chris loved it when the cavalry appeared and we would be joined by fifteen to twenty others who were all there to support him. Doing endless laps around the neighborhood was probably not their idea of a fascinating bike or run course, but they always made Chris feel that he was part of a team. On Sundays we would all meet at the lake at six o'clock in the morning to do his long runs.

There are a lot of ways to make a long bike ride fun. One way to reward a good workout is to celebrate and socialize, two of Chris's favorite activities. Since he does his longest rides on Saturdays with Dan and other members of the Tri Club, we'll often conclude an eight-hour bike ride with the whole gang going out to eat at Waffle House, Chris's favorite restaurant. As a reward for doing his personal best, he can have anything he wants. On Saturday nights Chris prefers to eat his big meal from P.F. Chang's alone. He finds whatever show happens to be his favorite that month on Netflix, pops in his earphones, and enjoys his meal while watching a show on his iPad. Like most adolescents, he prefers to spend his personal time alone. He doesn't even want us in the same room with him.

Training for an IRONMAN triathlon involves both intensive cardio and core strength development. When Chris and I first began training in the aftermath of his ear infections, he could only do a single push-up, sit-up, and squat. Using the 1% Better method, Chris slowly progressed to the point where he could do two hundred of each. This was in addition to lifting weights and other exercises designed to strengthen his core. (He is now up to three hundred, and by the 2021 IRONMAN World Championship triathlon in Hawaii, his goal is to be able to do five hundred push-ups, sit-ups, and squats.) We call these constant improvements Chris's "1% Better habit" as the improvement becomes automatic, an everyday habit that becomes quite easy through repetition.

Developing continuous improvements has another advantage over other ways of charting progress: it helps Chris avoid burning out. Burnout often takes place when people push themselves too much and too quickly. Sure, improving 5 percent a day would get Chris to two hundred reps faster, but could he actually do it? And if he did it, could he sustain it?

When Chris first started this journey, he didn't need an IRONMAN triathlete. He needed a friend who wasn't his parent. He needed somebody who was going to make things fun and with whom he could laugh and have a good time. Simone remains that to this day. She and Chris have spent countless hours together because they like to hang out. Having a friend like Simone helped to change Chris's life through his participation in Special Olympics and branching out into triathlons. Knowing that he would get to hang out with a friend during training motivated him. Simone's friendship also helped Chris learn the skills he needs to be a friend to somebody outside his family. Dan then became a second friend, as did his entire family. If you watch Dan and Chris now, you might think they've been best friends their entire lives, not just in the last year.

Until he met Simone, Dan, Hector, and others through his training, Chris didn't have friends who didn't themselves have disabilities. Chris had not experienced dynamics such as having an argument with a friend and needing to compromise or comforting somebody who was upset about something he had never experienced, like quitting a job or breaking up with a partner. He never had to tell somebody outside his family that he thought they were wrong or that what they were doing was unkind. He was not exposed to those experiences when he was sheltered within the family and community of other people with Down syndrome as he was when he became engaged within the larger community.

Chris has applied his lessons in friendship to get other people who have Down syndrome or those who are on the autism spectrum involved in triathlons. He convinced one of his best friends, Abigail, to join the Special Olympics triathlon team. As a result, Chris has a friend who is becoming a triathlete and learning to become more independent and involved in the wider community. With Chris spending much of his training time between Dan and me, Simone has become Abigail's Unified partner, even though she and Chris still work out together as well.

Chris's team has helped him make history and achieve something few people from any walk of life can achieve. In doing this, they have also welcomed Chris into a larger world where he is no longer isolated but is part of a circle of friends. This circle has wanted more than to help Chris run an IRONMAN race. His friends want him to be a productive part of a community and enjoy the warmth of human friendship and interaction. Chris talks to Simone, Dan, and Hector on the phone every night. They are a part of his circle that stretches beyond his family and into the greater world. His friends give him access to a world where people pay attention to him, where he gets to meet pretty women with whom he can flirt and look forward to seeing around town—the kinds of things many people take for granted.

I have heard Chris talking on the phone with Simone about her relationships or giving Dan a hard time about missing too many workouts after a night out with the guys. He gets to hear the back and forth of friends teasing each other or complaining about something or sharing private matters that only they and Chris know about. If this sounds normal, well, it is normal to most of us. But to Chris, these simple everyday interactions are manna from heaven that feeds his soul. Dan recently had a guys' weekend with a big group of former college chums. Chris was included in the weekend and reportedly had a blast. I don't know exactly what they did there. I guess what happens at the lake house stays at the lake house.

Dan always says that, in the final analysis, becoming an IRONMAN athlete is not about the fact that you crossed the finish line. It's about who you become in the process. It is the extra training in the heat and the cold, pushing yourself to get out of bed while the rest of the world sleeps comfortably, keeping yourself trim while everyone around you is drinking and eating delicious and unhealthy food. It's having to listen to people telling you that a 140.6-mile race is just plain crazy.

Chris hears some of that as well. So does the team we have built around him. The challenges—getting up to train, focusing more on what Chris needs than what we want to do—can get to all of us. We're not always on the same page, and sometimes we disagree over what to do. When this happens, we all remind ourselves of what, or rather who, brought us together. Four people who were strangers only a few years earlier have been drawn together by our common love for a remarkable young man. I am honored to have them on Team Chris.

9

"YOU ARE AN IRONMAN!"

After Chris finished the 2020 Olympic triathlon in January, I asked Dan whether he thought Chris could do an IRONMAN event.

"Absolutely," he said without missing a beat.

"Okay, let's give it a run," I replied. Then I gave Dan my little speech, sharing things I have learned from experience. "If we go on this journey, people are going to attack you. They're going to attack me. They're going say things about how unreasonable and even cruel we are. They are going to do it from a place of love and protection for Chris, but they are going to think we are going too far. What we have to do is trust that we're doing the right thing."

"Sure, no problem. I understand," Dan said. I could tell that he did not seem to entirely believe me, especially about the pushback we would get. As I mentioned earlier, Dan's own life experiences taught him to trust himself to overcome any barriers, and he saw no reason why Chris could not do the same. A man after my own heart.

As soon as we announced our plans, the whole world seemed to turn on us at once. This included our contacts at Special Olympics, the people we knew from the Tri Club, Chris's other coaches, and even his mom and sister. Their opposition to the notion of Chris doing an IRONMAN triathlon was the same as they vocalized when I proposed his doing an Olympic triathlon a year earlier. Sure, they loved seeing Chris making friends and getting incredibly fit, but did we have to kill him to do it?

They had a point. Finding precise statistics on the actual number of people who have competed in and finished an IRONMAN triathlon is difficult, as is trying to nail down the percentage of the world's population that participates in the events each year. According to Worldometer, there were approximately 7.5 billion people in the world in 2017,[1] which is the most recent year that participation in IRONMAN triathlons was tracked in full by Russ Cox on his sports data tracking website, CoachCox. Of these, CoachCox reported that approximately 80,000 people competed in an IRONMAN triathlon.[2] That represents 0.001 percent of the total population. Any triathlon poses a level of risk, and triathlons have claimed their share of lives, made all the more tragic as those who were lost were likely in the best shape of their lives. As recently as 2019, two men died during the swimming leg of an IRONMAN 70.3 triathlon in Madison, Wisconsin.

But their concern served mostly to confirm that we were

doing the right thing. Over the years, most of the success books and biographies I read had a common theme: significant success is achieved by people who go against the crowd. If everyone is going in one direction, you go the other way. I also learned that some of the greatest breakthroughs happen during the most difficult times. We were about to go against conventional thinking during a pandemic. In terms of significant historical events, this was going to be our version of the Great Depression and World War II.

Dan stuck to his guns and defended our plan, arguing that Chris could learn to become an IRONMAN competitor just like other athletes. Of course there were no more guarantees that Chris *could* do it than there were that anybody else could. We were not about to nip things in the bud in the service of my old nemesis "being realistic." Besides, Chris had been the first competitor with Down syndrome to complete an Olympic triathlon. Why would we possibly want to stop there?

Our first milestone would come May 9, 2020, at the COVID 70.3. The event was our defiance of COVID-19 consuming our society. We were going to take the race, which was half the distance of the ultra distance, head-on. The Central Florida Tri Club sponsored the race, which was more than twice as long as the Olympic triathlon Chris did in January. It would be a good test of where we stood with his training.

Chris and Dan did the event with some other members from the club. As this was not an officially sanctioned IRONMAN event, there were only about one hundred spectators, significantly fewer than the thousands that show up at official races. However, a local news station was on hand to capture the event, and several other media outlets picked up the story. Chris completed the COVID 70.3 triathlon in 8 hours and 25 minutes. If we extrapolated this to a full distance event, Chris's time would have been 16:50, keeping him under the maximum time of seventeen hours allowed for completing the race. *So far, so good*, I thought. Still, it was only half the distance, so we knew that if Chris wanted to maintain this pace at a full distance event, he had his work cut out for him between May and November.

I believe that God has a plan for every one of us, a plan He reveals to us in His own good time. If I had any doubts about whether God's plans for Chris included doing an IRONMAN triathlon on November 7, 2020, they ceased when the COVID-19 pandemic resulted in every full distance competition in the world being canceled except one: the Panama City Beach event set for November 7, 2020—the exact event for which Chris and Dan were signed up. I still get choked up when I think about the odds of this happening and what a profound blessing it was for Chris to be able to have a platform on which to show the fruits of his hard work. But, then again, the IRONMAN triathlon phenomenon has always produced wonderful examples of overcoming adversity.

◆ ◆ ◆

According to the IRONMAN website, "the single-day endurance event now known as IRONMAN was the brainchild of Judy and John Collins. . . . [who] participated in the Mission Bay Triathlon in San Diego on September 25, 1974.

[Although] that event now marks the start of the modern triathlon in the U.S.," the name *IRONMAN* was not applied to a triathlon until 1977, when the Collins family helped organize "a sprint run-swim competition in Honolulu," an event that inspired them to create something for the endurance athletes who "favored events such as the Waikiki Roughwater Swim and the Honolulu Marathon over short sprint events." After searching for a suitable route for bikes, the Collins couple landed on the idea of using a local cycling club's route. As legend has it, "Judy and John said to each other, 'If you do it, I'll do it,'" and John famously added, "Whoever finishes first, we'll call him the Iron Man."[3]

"At the Waikiki Swim Club banquet in October 1977, Judy and John announced their Around the Island Triathlon, to take place the following year. . . . On February 18, 1978, Judy and John Collins saw their dream come true with the first-ever Hawaiian Iron Man Triathlon." What began with a small group of endurance-sports enthusiasts in search of a new challenge gained worldwide recognition when the founders gave ABC's *Wide World of Sports* permission to film the event in 1980. Ever since then, the sport has seemed destined to produce iconic moments captured on tape, like in 1982, when "college student Julie Moss collapses just yards from the IRONMAN World Championship finish line." Although she was passed for the title, her crawl to the finish line sealed the event's brand as the ultimate triumph of the spirit.[4]

In 1997 the IRONMAN triathlon organizers recognized physically challenged athletes by awarding Australian John Maclean a World Championship trophy after he powered a hand-cycle bike and wheelchair across the finish line. As the

IRONMAN Group website explains, "Today, hundreds of thousands of triathletes from around the world have challenged themselves to prove to friends, loved ones, and even just themselves that 'Anything is Possible.'"[5]

◆ ◆ ◆

As you may recall, on the morning of the Panama City Beach event, the atmosphere was abuzz with athletes going through their warm-ups and spectators milling around. There may be nothing quite as lovely as a tropical breeze blowing off the Gulf of Mexico, but you see that breeze in a different light when you have to swim against it, which is precisely what Chris and Dan would be doing in their first leg.

Chris and Dan's warm-up exercises were a bit unusual due to the considerable numbers of athletes coming up to Chris to give him a hug and wish him luck. If well-wishers had been the only distraction, it would have been okay, but before long Chris had also attracted a posse of media representatives hoping to get a quick interview before the event. Dan did his best to make Chris as available as possible to the waves of well-wishers and media without letting them cut too deeply into warm-up and snack time.

For the first event, the swim, the athletes had to complete two circuits around the Russell-Fields Pier, totaling just shy of 2.5 miles. The two circuits were very sensibly designed to group athletes based on their estimated swim times, ensuring those of similar abilities were competing side by side while those of lesser ability didn't have to worry about constantly being overtaken by stronger swimmers. The waters in the

Gulf typically hover in the low seventies, so swimmers were allowed to wear wet suits, which Chris and Dan both did.

The course used the universal buoy system to keep swimmers on track, and boats were posted at regular intervals to rescue anybody who signaled they needed help. Competitors had 1 hour and 10 minutes to complete the first loop and 2 hours and 20 minutes to complete the entire swim course. If they couldn't hit these times, they were allowed to continue to the next discipline but were designated DNF—did not finish—at the day's end. Once they hit the turquoise waters of the Gulf, their race began, and they had seventeen hours to finish it.

◆ ◆ ◆

Dan had fixed a black bungee cord to Chris for added safety in what they expected to be crowded waters. As it turned out, that proved to be a good move because Chris and Dan actually went with the first wave of swimmers, the professional women. Chris and Dan emerged from their second loop in a little under two hours after they started, within the time limit set by IRONMAN regulations. Dan quickly removed the bungee cord from Chris, and they jogged over to the bike area. Chris is unable to start or stop the bike by himself, so Dan helped him onto his bike, and they headed out for a 112-mile ride, stopping every thirty minutes so Chris could hydrate.

The bike course started on Pier Park Drive and followed some rolling hills, crossing over the Intracoastal Waterway before returning along Front Beach Road. As I mentioned earlier, during one of the stops, Chris stepped on a mound of red fire ants and was badly stung. Dan was forced into some fast makeshift medical attention but not before several of the red devils found a way to lodge themselves beneath Chris's time chip, from which location they continued to torment him.

When Chris and Dan got back into the race, they found the course was becoming very hilly. Moreover, the road was twisting, which made navigation for Chris rather difficult. Dan was riding just off of Chris's left flank and shouting instructions to him as he pedaled his way through this part of the course. I can just hear Dan: "Break here." "Turn here." "Coast here." "Pedal here." At about the 50-mile mark, I met Chris and the team, gave them some medication for the ant stings, anti-itch cream, and a much-needed hug. Our reunion served to boost Chris's spirits, and he immediately took off faster than ever on his bike. I was following them a short way back on a motor scooter that Dan had rented for me. From my vantage point, I could see Dan trying to get Chris to slow down. Chris hadn't brought his hearing aid to the event, so not hearing Dan's instructions, he continued to barrel down the winding hills.

At one point, you'll remember, Chris hit a rough patch in the road and lost control of the bike. His front wheel went sideways, and the back of his bike flipped, tossing Chris over his bike. He landed hard but proceeded to execute a somersault and popped up as though he had been trained to do so at some elite Army Ranger camp. It was incredible. He actually flexed his biceps, as if to say, *No problem!*

Sometimes it is harder to watch something happen than

to participate in the "happening" yourself. That must surely have been the case with Chris's fall. When Dan and I got to him, we were expecting the worst. Had he broken his wrist? Worse . . . a concussion? Imagine our relief when we reached him and found him standing there laughing and telling the whole world, "I just crashed my bike! I just crashed my bike!"

We patched up Chris's bloody knee, and as Chris and Dan resumed the race, we realized that while Chris was still safely inside the cutoff time for the overall event and on the bike course, he was behind on our plan of allowing extra time for the marathon, which was not his strongest event. The crash and ant attack had wasted time that he needed to make up. At mile 80 we had a little roadside regrouping, and I explained to Chris that he needed to ride his bike faster than he ever had in his life—in training or in races. Although he usually averages fifteen to sixteen miles an hour, he pushed his speed to twenty to twenty-five miles an hour for over 30 miles. Accounting for rest and nutrition breaks, he maintained a pace of seventeen to eighteen miles an hour, which was just below average for a typical triathlete. I can't say enough good things about the endless stream of athletes who shouted encouragements to Chris and Dan as they made up their lost time and bested the cutoff by eight minutes.

On to the marathon.

Dan had chosen to retether Chris to help him keep his pace and stay on course. Against the backdrop of the Gulf shoreline, Chris and Dan made their way through the night-time darkness. At one point they passed us in the crowd, and we cheered them with all our might. But after ten miles of running, Chris began to show the unmistakable signs of hitting the wall: his eyes were glazed over, he was as white as a sheet, and his stride was shortening by the minute. Dan tried some techniques to get Chris over the hump, such as mixing up six minutes of walking with one minute of running to keep Chris from giving up entirely. It wasn't working. I met them at the 11-mile mark, and we tried to figure out a plan.

I wanted to see whether it would help if Dan removed the tether. Dan is a very strong-willed individual, so I know it took a tremendous act of will for him not to press his points more forcefully to keep the tether in place. Dan is also Chris's "adopted uncle" and, next to me, the closest male in Chris's life. I knew he disagreed with every fiber of his being about removing Chris's tether, but he deferred to me and removed it. Dan considered it a sign of giving up and that the race was over. Instead, it gave Chris a win so he felt in control.

We walked and ran together without the tether for a couple of miles until we reached the end of the first loop. That's when I knew everything was going to be okay. Chris is used to thinking in loops around the neighborhood. Even though this loop was 13 miles, it was the last loop. In Chris's mind, the race was practically over because he had only one more loop. Earlier I mentioned that as the head coach, my focus with the 1% Better approach was on building Chris's mind. This is an example of that. Once Chris decided in his mind that he had just one more loop, he was then able to get his body to buy into it and get him to the end.

It was at that point I told Chris about the battle between his dreams and his fake pain, and he replied that his dreams were "going to win." It was the most critical part of the race and the point of the 1% Better strategy. My entire focus was to help Chris build a strong mind, one that would always anchor on his dreams and get stronger as he got closer to the end. It worked. I turned the rest of the race back over to Dan, Chris's guardian angel, to bring Chris across the finish line in the best way he knew.

To their infinite credit, Dan and Chris chose to give it their all even though this was one of the flattest run courses on the IRONMAN triathlon circuit. They were not doing the event to barely finish but to put in their best effort, come what may. Someday another person with Down syndrome is going to cross that finish line. The last thing we would want is for them to have an easy time breaking Chris's record or to think that it is enough to stagger over the finish line.

Chris crossed the finish line with arms held high in celebration and a little time to spare. All the people who supported him during those crazy eleven months leading up to the event, as well as those who supported him before that, met him at the finish line. There were hugs aplenty and more tears than you could measure. But they were joyous tears.

Chris's achievement landed him on the Guinness World Records list as the first athlete with Down syndrome to complete a full distance IRONMAN triathlon. Special Olympics named Chris as one of its Champion Ambassadors, whose charge is to advocate for its mission, to "amplify the message of inclusion to smash barriers, unite people, and ultimately put people of all abilities on a level playing field."[6] Chris's fellow Champion Ambassadors include the actress Lily D. Moore, renowned photographer Nigel Barker, Jamaican Olympic swimmer Alia Atkinson, singer-songwriter Montell

Jordan, and professional football players Eddie Yarbrough, Dalton Risner, and Mack Hollins.

The Champion Ambassadors are joined by a cohort of Global Ambassadors that include professional wrestler Paul Wight ("Big Show"); baseball all-stars Gleyber Torres and Willson Contreras; Olympic swimming legend Michael Phelps; Olympic champion figure skater Michelle Kwan; professional basketball stars Andre Drummond, Damian Lillard, Devin Booker, Ricky Rubio, Elena Delle Donne, Sam Perkins, and Dikembe Mutombo; soccer stars Didier Drogba and Cafu; and golfer Pádraig Harrington.

When we came back from the IRONMAN event, Special Olympics Florida held an event in Chris's honor in Clermont. The governor made an appearance, as did the local media.

Special Olympics Florida conferred the title of Local Hero on Chris for his achievements. And then Special Olympics representatives announced that they had another surprise for him: Special Olympics USA championships were going to include a triathlon in 2022, and Chris and his team were the first athletes invited to compete.

◆ ◆ ◆

The late Sir Roger Bannister is an example I have often used for the possibilities of human achievement. On May 6, 1954, Bannister was a twenty-five-year-old medical student who became the first person to officially break through the fabled four-minute-mile barrier. Running with the help of two pacers, Bannister clocked a 3:59.4 mile over four laps of the cinder track at Iffley Road, Oxford. In doing so, he became a symbol of human achievement that resonated far beyond the world of athletics.

At the time, Bannister's barrier-breaking race stood as a positive symbol after the world emerged from two destructive wars into a new dawn of heroic aspiration. It now stands with the achievements of the Wright brothers, the conquest of Everest, and the first man on the moon.[7]

Australian runner John Landy, only forty-six days after Bannister made history, beat that record by more than a second. Morocco's Hicham El Guerrouj is today's current men's mile record holder with a time of 3:43.13.

Bannister spent the rest of his life politely denying that his sub-four-minute mile was so significant and assiduously built a career that he valued more highly in medicine and neurological research.

On the sixty-seventh anniversary of his achievement, Bannister's 3:59.4 mile still resonates and remains a landmark achievement for runners. "We run, not because we think it is doing us good, but because we enjoy it and cannot help ourselves," Bannister said. "The more restricted our society and work become, the more necessary it will be to find some outlet for this craving for freedom. No one can say, 'You must not run faster than this or jump higher than that.' The human spirit is indomitable."[8]

When I see the iconic black-and-white photograph of Bannister crossing the finish line, I think of Chris's photo at the finish line of Visit Panama City Beach IRONMAN Florida triathlon. Both athletes have the same look of utter exhaustion, which, at the very moment of victory, has been transmuted into the sheer, unbridled ecstasy that lies within all of us.

Chris may never attain Bannister-like achievements, but he will be 1 percent better at something today than he was yesterday. Ultimately he will get closer and closer to being the best version of himself. One day he will be playing in a golf tournament, and the next day he'll be playing pick-up basketball at the gym. Another day might find him acting in a commercial, playing the piano for his girlfriend, competing in the New York City Marathon, or working toward another IRONMAN World Championship in Kona, Hawaii.

He is on his own journey, one in which he enjoys every day and feels successful every day.

Can you imagine living a life where success is measured by being a little better today at something than you were yesterday?

Wow, what a life.

PART 3

GETTING TO 1% BETTER

This book celebrates Chris's achievement and offers a blueprint for others who want to overcome the obstacles in their lives to achieve their goals and dreams. To understand this crazy and wonderful journey that all of us who love Chris have been on with him, you have to understand the concept of 1% Better. This idea was the result of years of reading and learning from other people—of teaching myself how to get better by teaching others how to get better and by applying business principles to help Chris discover his dreams and develop a set of goals to reach them.

As I've mentioned before, I would date the sea change in my thinking, motivation, and achievement to the weekend Patty and I spent with Coach John Wooden. During our meals, car rides, and the downtime we spent with the great coach, I was struck by the gap I felt between my perception of Wooden, the legendary champion, and the humble man Patty and I were charged with chaperoning. Even more than this, Wooden himself fleshed things out when he answered my fanboy questions about what it felt like to win so many championships. He did not emphasize how it felt. Instead, he talked about how long it took him to win his first championship.

Wooden disapproved of the misperception that he was an overnight success. "What they don't know is that I worked for fifteen years before anybody heard of me. I worked to improve slowly," he told us.

The improvements Coach Wooden made from day to day and week to week were often so insignificant that he couldn't tell if his techniques were improving the team or not. The key, he told us, was strictly a matter of perspective. "It was when I looked at my coaching over a longer period—over several years, in fact—that I could see where improvements had begun to creep in and change our rate of success," he told us.

It was not hard to understand why Wooden was the perfect keynote speaker for an Amway meeting. The Amway model requires you to start slowly and build your networks. In the first year or so, you are likely to make little or no progress. It starts by finding the first person to sponsor, then the second, then the twentieth. The momentum kicks in when you teach them to sponsor others and the compounding effect takes place. Your network grows to hundreds, then thousands of others whose success you helped create and also get to share.

One of the most famous ambassadors Amway ever produced was a man named Dexter Yager. He was an average man from Rome, New York, who became a millionaire many times over by patiently cultivating his network over many years. When he grew famous enough to be in demand as a motivational speaker, people asked him to divulge his success secrets. He told them to dream big. That was it. That was his big idea. If you had a big dream, you could do anything. Yager wanted to get rich, but he did not believe that getting rich *quickly* offered most people a practical model. So he always returned to the importance of dreaming big: success was about keeping your dream front and center and letting everything else take care of itself. Much like Wooden's idea of slow, incremental improvement, Yager's emphasis on cultivating and nurturing a big dream guided the work Chris and I did. (I explore this in detail in the appendix.)

Several years ago I wrote a white paper on the concept of "leading, leaning, and lagging" metrics in sales that was eventually published in 2016 in a book called *The Road to Success*. (Note: Please bear with me here. This rather arcane subject matter *did* influence how Chris and I managed his development in triathlons—I promise.) In my article I compared sales metrics to baseball. Specifically, I had in mind the excellent book *Moneyball: The Art of Winning an Unfair Game*, Michael Lewis's case study in understanding the power of leveraging the right metrics. The basic premise of *Moneyball* is that a hundred years of devoted baseball statistics had never truly been optimized until someone started looking at them differently.

That someone was Billy Beane, the longtime general manager for the Oakland Athletics. He discovered that the most critical metric in baseball was the on-base percentage. Beane leveraged this metric to try something that nobody had ever attempted before in baseball. With the second-lowest payroll in the league, he put together a team of misfits—using this one metric of on-base percentage—to identify undervalued talent for his goal of winning without spending. That team ended up as a constant contender in the American League despite a low payroll, and Beane's new moneyball methodology changed baseball forever.

Let me illustrate by using the moneyball example. Beane's goal was to win enough games to make the playoffs. To achieve this, he needed to improve three key performance indicators, or KPIs. The KPI metrics were:

1. number of at-bats (activities)
2. on-base percentage (outcomes)
3. number of runs per game (results)

By improving those three KPIs, the Oakland As went from last to first and into the playoffs.

I first began talking about the 1% Better concept during sales training presentations that I made to corporate clients. In sales there are dozens of KPI metrics. I focused on three. If a company wanted to increase sales by 10 to 20 percent in ninety days and build a continuous-improvement system, they needed to improve in these KPI metrics:

1. Meaningful conversations (activities)
2. Deals created (outcomes)
3. Win-rate percent (results)

By increasing each of these three metrics a little bit, you get a big increase in sales. Let me drill down a bit.

For example, the first metric should involve the number of meaningful conversations a salesperson has with clients and prospects. Perhaps that equates to having one hundred conversations over a ninety-day period. The second metric involves the conversion rate of those conversations to opportunities. In people terms this means asking, of the one hundred people you talked to, how many had a good enough experience to consider buying your product or service, or how many of them resulted in uncovering one new opportunity. If the answer is ten, you have a 10 percent conversion ratio. The third and final ratio looks at the rate of how many of those ten opportunities you actually win. If you win three, you have a 30 percent win ratio.

When speaking to an audience of sales professionals, I would always ask, "Do you believe it's reasonable and possible to increase each of these metrics by 1 percent?" Then I would get very specific so they understood the question. "Let's say we go from 100 to 101 conversations, from 10 percent to 11 percent in terms of opportunities generated, and from 30 percent to 31 percent in closed opportunities. Is that reasonable?" Undoubtedly everyone would say, "Of course, yes, we believe that is reasonable and possible." This is a crucial step in building the 1% Better habit. People have to believe it's reasonable and possible. If they do, they will act on that and their chance of success skyrockets. If they don't believe it's reasonable and possible, they won't act on it and be successful. As Theodore Roosevelt is often credited with having said, "Believe you can and you're halfway there." Similarly, American industrialist Henry Ford is famously credited as having said, "Whether you think you can or you think you can't—you're right."

"Okay," I would continue, "then how much of an increase in revenues would that 1 percent improvement generate?" Calculators would be whipped out, and people would say 3 percent or 4 percent.

"No, the answer is 15 percent." Then, I would show them the numbers. The calculators would come out again, and, after a moment, everybody in the room would be blown away. What they had not figured into their thinking was the power of compounding, in which small, incremental changes early on grow exponentially into large changes later.

This is the power of incremental improvements, compounded.

◆ ◆ ◆

When Chris started participating in Special Olympics Triathlon, it was just to get in shape and meet some people. It was something Chris and I wanted to do together. Before that, I was so busy with work that I wasn't spending much time with him or Patty. I was just in survival mode, trying to make enough money to take care of my family should something happen to me. I had come to accept that Chris would never be able to take care of himself and would need to pay others to take care of him for the rest of his life. And I assumed Patty would live into her nineties, like her mom, so the financial burden fell on me. My only answer was to build a company, sell it, and have enough money to care for them for the next thirty years.

Since I have always believed that God has a plan, my job is to roll with it. I don't usually ask why because the answer is generally too complicated for me to understand. I only trust God and roll with it. "Your will be done" remains the last thing I say every night before I go to bed.

During our neighborhood runs and bike rides, lots of other families were always out and about, kids playing in their yards or moms walking together and pushing strollers. I was happy to be enjoying the beautiful outdoors with Chris instead of having him cooped up inside watching TV or playing video games, which I see as dead-end pastimes. The longer a child sits in front of those screens, the harder it is to pry the child away. I was happy we had started Chris early on with golf and track. On our rides Chris and I became competitive, as parents and children sometimes do for fun while biking. We often concluded our rides with Chris trying to beat me. These were fun times, and I wanted to make our races as fun as possible, but racing with Chris could be a little hair-raising because he would respond by going faster and faster while I still had to look out ahead for cars and people.

Sometimes when we had done forty laps and found ourselves in the zone, I would look over at him and see the wheels turning in his mind and his growing feeling of mastery on the road. Through repetition and subconscious memory, he was learning how to make split-second decisions as he executed turns riding twenty or thirty miles an hour or while straining to go uphill at seven miles an hour. I proudly watched him shift gears, keeping the right distance between himself and me and others in the neighborhood, and evading a car that was slowly backing down a driveway toward him. He used every second to learn something from his environment.

He learned these things over and over again until repetition became reflex.

There is an old saying that "necessity is the mother of invention." Chris and I put the wisdom of this adage to the test in the watershed year of 2019, when I found it necessary to devise a novel way to help Chris reach a new level in his workouts. I began to think that a good way of going about this would be to apply business principles to Chris's life. Our goal would be to get Chris into Special Olympics USA Games in 2022, which were to be held in Orlando. Training for a triathlon was the perfect opportunity to help Chris get in shape, make friends, and have a goal to shoot for.

Chris's lack of success in the Special Olympics state championships in August 2019 and the USA Games' decision to cancel the triathlon were devastating because even if Chris wasn't yet good enough, now he seemed left without a goal. But when he swam across Lake Cane in Lucky's Lake Swim in October 2019, it was a huge achievement for him. I'll never forget, after Chris swam across the lake that first time, how he signed his name on the wall at Lucky Meisenheimer's house: "Chris World Champion." Keeping an eye on God's signs, I looked at that and said to Chris, "Why not? Why can't you do something extraordinary that would make you a world champ?"

We were still focused on getting 1 percent better even though we had no goal to shoot for, such as competing in the USA Games. So I started thinking. There were hundreds, maybe thousands, of such sprint races going on around the country at the time. If we looked at Chris's time in the race and compared it to others going on, Chris probably would have finished in the bottom 0.0001 percent of all the people in the world doing the same kind of race. So when we say that God uses the least likely among us to deliver a message, all you have to do is look at the race results and know that if God was going to use one person from this group to deliver a powerful global message, He would pick Chris.

God may have put us on the road to doing an IRONMAN triathlon, but it was people like John Wooden, Dexter Yager, and Billy Beane who gave us the road map to get there. Each in his varied way—Wooden and Yager through their philosophies and Beane through his upending of conventional wisdom—convinced me that we had nothing to lose by trying. So we did.

Chris has taught me that you have to believe something is possible before you attempt it. When there is no belief, no amount of hope lingering in the back of your mind will push over the barrier to achievement. And once we all got on this journey, it became more and more obvious to me that Chris's journey could become something that would help other kids with special needs become a more inclusive part of their communities, something that showed them they could achieve so much more if they worked for it in the right way and right frame of mind. Each time I set the bar higher for Chris, he has gotten over it with room to spare. And he has done things that never were attempted before because nobody ever thought they were possible.

Reaching a goal starts with belief. Ironically, I began applying business principles to Chris's training, but eventually I started circling back and applying Chris's IRONMAN journey to business coaching. Today Chris's story informs

everything I do. "Look," I told a roomful of sales professionals in Orlando a year ago, "you know this 1% Better stuff I'm
teaching you? Well, I've had my son doing this for six months
on his journey to doing a triathlon."

◆ ◆ ◆

Patty and I were entering a new phase in our lives, one that we
had not anticipated or planned for but for which God clearly
did have a plan. Maybe God wanted me to learn and perfect the
1% Better concept with professional salespeople before trying
it on my son. Perhaps He wanted my head to be so full of 1%
Better that I could not help but think of applying it with Chris.
If I regret anything, it is that I did not understand the concept
earlier so that I could have applied it to Jacky's development
as an athlete. She did plenty well with the tools she had at her
disposal, but could she have accomplished even more if she had
taken the approach Chris had? I think she would have.

Maybe I needed to go through the whole process of learning about the leading, leaning, and lagging metrics and how
to start measuring things. Maybe I needed to stop looking
at the world the way most people do and start looking at it
through numbers in order to see something that nobody else
was seeing. Kind of like moneyball. It took a numbers guy, not
a baseball guy, to figure it out. Ten years ago I would not have
been capable of helping Chris accomplish what he has done. I
began charting a graph (which I share with you in chapter 13)
and was able to see the correlation between Chris's training
and the irrefutable gains he was making over time.

But I knew what I knew and did what I did, and somehow

I got smarter over time. And maybe God wanted us to be an example so we could teach other parents like us; other siblings, like Jacky; and other members of the community, like Dan and Hector, how to change the perception of the community about what is possible.

11

LESSONS FOR ACHIEVING A 1% BETTER MINDSET

I would never claim to have invented the idea of gradual, persistent improvement or even 1 percent improvement. The concept has been around for a long time. But what I do claim credit for is the way I applied it to helping my son, Chris, accomplish what most people thought impossible. In this chapter I will highlight how I have come to think about the 1% Better mindset through my work with Chris, and in the following chapter I will offer some practical lessons I learned that may be applied by others in their own lives.

The first thing to know about this mindset is that it is perfectly *counterintuitive*. Today's culture worships high-profile overachievers who promote quick fixes and the conviction that where there is no pain, there is no gain. I think this philosophy is hogwash. The "no pain, no gain" mindset is not only unpleasant but also ineffective and even pernicious to sustainable improvement. It leads to burnout and backsliding for all but the small fraction of the population who have the physical, emotional, or intellectual capacity for accelerating peak performance in the shortest possible time. Most of us are average, and Chris was below average, and it is for us that 1% Better is designed.

A short story will illustrate.

As this book was coming together, our daughter, Jacky, asked me to explain exactly what I meant by 1% Better. I answered by asking her who our educational and athletic systems of achievement were designed for. Were they for the most socially, intellectually, and athletically disadvantaged? Were they for the top 1 percent of the population in terms of talent, drive, opportunity, or some other measure? Or were they for the rest of us, the also-rans who comprise the vast majority of the population?

Jacky thought for a minute and answered the higher end of the rest of us. After all, the top 1 percent, whether it is somebody like Bill Gates or LeBron James, is going to succeed no matter what obstacles are thrown in their way. Conventional limits bore them, and these folks usually come to our attention because they wind up doing things that are completely new. These are the elite, and to be honest, Jacky falls into this category.

These are not the people our education and athletic systems are set up to serve. They are set up to serve the rest of us, the 99 percent who range from very talented and high achieving to subpar and low achieving. Our educational system is set up to sort the rest of us, taking us from one phase to another:

from elementary school to middle school to high school to college and, finally, to a career. Similarly, our athletic systems are set up to create pathways to follow through youth sports programs that become more and more competitive and elite.

For example, I gave Jacky a scenario. Let's say there are ten thousand girls your age who live in greater Orlando. (That's a reasonable number.) Every year ten of those girls are selected to play on the girls' elite travel basketball team. In effect, this means that the girls' basketball development is set up to identify and prepare a tiny fraction of elite players who will go on to play college sports. The rest of the population is welcome to do the best it can, but the system limits them by its very structure, which is to compete for a place in the hierarchy. The high achievers will occupy executive positions in companies and other industries, the large group of average achievers will work their tails off trying to provide for their families, and the lowest achievers will grow increasingly dependent on the system to provide for them.

Now imagine the effect this system would have on somebody of average ability, let alone somebody like Chris. They're trying to compete with a group of people who intellectually and physically are more advanced and are very likely to resign themselves to limiting what they believe they can achieve—*to know their place in the great lineup of life*. And they often learn this lesson early on in life, which dampens their motivation to push themselves harder. Chris had gotten nowhere after eighteen years in those traditional systems because those systems weren't designed to help him maximize his potential but to become dependent on those further up the ladder of traditional success.

But guess what? I think that more of us can do better in school, in sports, and in life if we look outside traditional systems of education and sports. What if we reframed a system for those people who don't have the intellectual and physical capacity to compete in the current system? I emphasize the word *compete* because the key to the traditional system lies in competition: the traditional system is a zero-sum game in which everybody vies for a limited number of places. But what would happen if, instead of viewing competition as a zero-sum game of one against all, we viewed it as a game of me against myself? Me against my natural human instinct to push myself to keep getting better at something so I can reach my goals and dreams? I can tell you what happened when Chris and I reframed his approach from traditional to 1% Better: he went from being a couch potato who was forty pounds overweight and dealing with the extraordinary physical and intellectual challenges of living with Down syndrome to becoming an IRONMAN triathlete.

The key to understanding and using the 1% Better mindset in your own life is to recognize that it is, first and foremost, a mindset. For example, if I wanted to lose fifty pounds, I would not focus on losing fifty pounds because that is the result of the mindset, not the mindset itself. If I adopt the 1% Better mindset, the pounds will come off because the body will follow the mind's lead when the messages are reinforced over and over again. The first thing I would do is to write down my dreams related to losing weight. Your dream is the first crucial step. The dream motivating my weight-loss goals would tap into the deepest reasons for wanting to lose the weight. Maybe I'm tired of being tired all the time or of people making fun of me. Maybe I want to be healthy enough to enjoy taking long walks with my wife without worrying about collapsing. Maybe I want to be able to play with my grandchildren. Maybe it's all of these things.

But none of my goals will motivate me if I don't write them down where I can see them every day. So I create a dream board that serves as my true north to keep me on the straight path toward achieving them. That's why Chris wrote his dreams down on the wall of his bedroom and read them every morning when he woke up and before he went to sleep—marrying somebody like his mom, driving a car, owning a home. They had nothing to do with being able to complete an IRONMAN triathlon.

Next, to achieve my dreams of better health and vigor, I would set goals that could be far out enough to be achievable and yet close enough to keep me motivated. Goals are the means to reaching your dream and will come and go—on average, goals will change every three or four months—but a dream goes on forever. You can expand your dream or tweak it in other ways, but it is the life you want to lead. Chris had a dream that required large goals, but your dreams and goals need not be so large.

Once you have established your goals, you need a plan to reach them. Your plan would include milestones or markers that you seek to hit. If you're driving from Orlando to Miami, you would see mile markers along the highway letting you know if you're headed in the right direction at the pace you set for yourself. With Chris, we knew he had to prepare to go from running an Olympic triathlon in January to an

IRONMAN triathlon in November. That enabled us to put markers in place leading up to the final goal.

Let's return to our weight-loss example. If your goal of supporting your healthy-lifestyle dream required you to lose fifty pounds, you wouldn't focus on the fifty pounds. That would be too frustrating and demotivating. But what if your plan was to lose one pound a week? That would break down to a couple of ounces a day that could be achieved by not eating a cookie after dinner and increasing your exercise time by a small fraction each day. Using this plan, you would lose fifty pounds in fifty weeks, or around twelve and a half months. That may seem like a long time, but it's a drop in the bucket compared to how long it took you to build up to your present condition, right? Your progress would be nearly imperceptible to you as your energy level gradually increased, your sleep improved, and your favorite pants fit again.

But here is the key point: the most important thing that will have changed is your mindset, not your weight. The reason so many diets fail is that they focus on the body without training the mind. So when the strict and difficult diet regimen is over, the mind has not developed good habits to live by, and usually within a year, weight gain creeps back on. In the 1% Better example, however, the mind has become okay with eating slightly less and exercising a little more each day. It has formed an achievement habit that you can sustain for the rest of your life.

When you develop the ability to become 1% Better—to develop an achievement habit—you can apply it to anything you want. It doesn't need to end with weight loss. With Chris, we are applying it to his love of golf and playing the piano, both of which are activities that are difficult for most people to learn and terribly hard for those with Down syndrome. But he is improving in both of these activities and may someday become a golfer who breaks 70.

But what about you? How would you apply your achievement habit to other areas of life? One area that most students want to improve is their performance in school. It is a key avenue to going to college and succeeding, then going on to get a well-paying job that provides a great living and esteem in the community. The problem is that, at present, you are a student who gets mostly Cs or Ds.

How do you change that?

Well, first you write down the details of your dream of going to college, maybe a very selective one, and thriving there. Then you give yourself a year to establish a new mindset, one in which you increase the amount of time you study between school and dinner from zero minutes to one minute. The next day, or by whatever schedule you set, you increase it to two minutes and then three minutes and then four minutes. You have a goal of increasing your GPA by a full point or a point and a half, but you're probably not going to see your grades changing much in the first semester. However, there's a good chance you will see at least one of your grades improve—perhaps for a subject you like more than the others. And in nine to twelve months, or in about two to three school terms, you will be studying and achieving at a rate needed to earn grades that will get you into college or raise your GPA for admission into that selective university you want to attend.

Remember, getting As is not your purpose. Developing

the mindset of achievement is what you're after. The As will eventually come. The moment you develop this 1% Better habit, you will find yourself applying it to other things, and improving your grades will shift to improving your body, your golf game, your guitar-playing, and so forth. After you finish reading this book, pick an area in your life in which to develop an achievement mindset. You don't have to begin with anything monumental or serious. Any area will do for learning how to develop the mindset; then apply it to other areas of your life.

◆ ◆ ◆

To help you get started, allow me to share some of the key lessons I picked up working with Chris. They included these:

1. Compelling gap
2. Learning curve and style
3. Dream board
4. 1% Better *together*
5. Weekly cadence call
6. Motivation

As you can see, there are quite a few lessons, and most are interrelated; for example, having a weekly cadence call will support your effort to be 1% Better together. Staying motivated depends on matching the right learning curve and style to the individual rather than trying to shoehorn somebody into a one-size-fits-all template. Let's take the lessons up one by one.

COMPELLING GAP. In sales one of the most important first steps I take is the identification of what I call a "compelling gap," which means showing the gap between the current situation and the desired one. With Chris, the gap was enormous. For example, at the start of Chris's IRONMAN journey, he could barely balance himself on a bike. (Most kids are riding a bike by the time they are five or six; Chris was sixteen when he first learned.) His muscle tone was not as developed as most people his age, even those who are sedentary. His learning curve was also slower than average. It took him hours to learn what others were able to learn in minutes.

Without going into excessive detail, these basic hurdles created numerous technical problems with operating a bike in race conditions that included sitting, peddling, hydration, nutrition, aerodynamics, and every facet of cycling. When I added up additional physical and mental hurdles Chris had to clear above the race requirements themselves, I estimated he had to expend between 60 and 80 percent more energy than typical athletes. The gap Chris had to close between himself and IRONMAN triathlon requirements designed for typical athletes was considerable indeed!

LEARNING CURVE AND STYLE. As I noted earlier in the chapter, there's a world full of people who don't fit into the system that was designed to sort out the top 1 percent of high achievers and the "best of the rest" from everybody else. Popular belief notwithstanding, this system is not designed for you to do the best that you can do; it's designed to measure what you can do alongside everybody else. The 1% Better method, by contrast, is all about setting up a process that lets you do the best you can do. This requires that you adjust your habit formation to account for the way you learn and the speed at which you learn.

Instead of trying to compare yourself to others, which is where the whole system falls apart, you stop looking at other people and look only at yourself, taking satisfaction from becoming a better version of you. Everybody can be success-ful because they're comparing themselves today against themselves yesterday.

Not only should you feel okay about learning at a different rate than other people, but you should also feel good about learning differently. Chris was unable to understand the con-cept of measurements that typical people do. So instead of teaching him how to shift gears based on mileage—a com-mon practice among cyclists—we applied sidewalk chalk every one hundred yards that told him when to shift gears. If you find yourself teaching somebody who doesn't learn the way you do, remember what John Wooden said about teaching: you haven't taught until they have learned.

DREAM BOARD. The key first step to making the 1% Better method work is to create a dream board that focuses and aligns your deepest feelings and your conscious thoughts and acts. The best literature I have read, includ-ing James Clear's influential *Atomic Habits*, shows that we are more likely to develop good habits when they result in the fulfillment of a powerful goal or dream. The dream furnishes the motivation for developing and maintaining the habits. It also serves as a filter, allowing you to say no to whatever does not help you reach your dream.

When Chris and I began our IRONMAN challenge, I knew that he would need something powerful to motivate him through the long journey ahead—on foot, on a bike, and in the water. Signing his name "Chris World Champion" showed that he wanted to do something great. Still, that goal needed a more encompassing dream, a deep desire that would not end when he crossed a finish line. This is why, on New Year's Eve 2019, I gave Chris a dream board and a marker and asked him to write down his dreams. I documented this with a video as he was doing it. He wrote these exact words:

1. Buy my own car
2. Buy my own house
3. Get a smoky-hot blond wife from Minnesota
4. Have my own money to take care of my family
5. Be a famous public speaker
6. Be a successful businessman

When I tried to tease more out of him, he simply said, "Like you, Dad."

At some point in their lives, many sons dream of emulating their fathers. They usually outgrow these feelings as they become more independent. With Chris, the independence is taking much longer to attain, which explains how a twenty-year-old would still be able to dream that nothing could be better than living a life just like his dad's. And for a young man with Down syndrome, that would be a fantastic accomplishment indeed.

As I said earlier, goals are the means to realizing a dream. Goals are finite and subject to change. Dreams are endless and grow. When Chris achieved his goal of completing an IRONMAN triathlon, he created a new goal of competing in the IRONMAN World Championship. After you have achieved your goal of losing fifty pounds, you may want to create a goal of running road races, then running them under a certain time, and finally winning a race in your age bracket.

The motivation that will keep you in that goal-setting and goal-achieving frame of mind is your dream board, which you will interact with every day. Once you've crossed the mid-point in your timeline for a goal, something magical happens: you get more and more excited because you see the board fill up with the activities you have already done and—yay!—you are getting closer to your next milestone.

1% BETTER *TOGETHER*. As evidenced by Team Chris, developing lifelong achievement isn't something most of us can accomplish alone. We all need at least one accountability partner, a person we trust to hold us to our commitments and insist on helping us become our best selves. We want some-body who won't back down because they are afraid of losing our friendship. That is why parents can be such great part-ners: they have their children's best interests in mind, know their children better than anybody, and can spend more time with them than others can. However, I am not suggesting that friends or siblings cannot also be excellent accountability partners, as long as they are willing to provide support when things are going badly as well as when things are breezing along nicely.

WEEKLY CADENCE CALL. Whether you are trying to get 1 percent better in partnership with one other person or with several people, I have found that the best way to ensure you are all pulling in the same direction is to have a weekly "cadence call." *Cadence* refers to things we do regularly and the rhythms of activity we establish in our lives. A cadence call, then, keeps track of our weekly rhythms as they pertain to a specific set of activities, such as training for an IRONMAN triathlon. A cadence call is basically a way to touch base to evaluate the previous week and plan the next week. You can do it by phone, by video conference, or live. The cadence call should include every member of your accountability team. In Chris's case, this call takes place every Sunday evening at seven o'clock and lasts for half an hour. It includes Dan, Simone, and Hector.

During the call, we share what everybody did the week before. "Hey, did you run into any problems?" "What did you accomplish?" "What did you achieve?" "Where did we fall short, and how can we make up time?" Then we plan for the next week and adjust as necessary. The beauty of a cadence call is that it allows you to adjust in real time to ensure you stay on track. Plan a week at a time to keep everything fresh and flexible.

MOTIVATION. People often ask me whether Chris was born with a lot of motivation to accomplish extraordinary things, such as complete IRONMAN events. I tell them the truth, which is that it is far more likely that Chris was born with a strong motivation to sit on the couch and play video games. In fact, I would say that Chris's innate motivation was probably at the lower end of the bell curve, somewhere in the bottom 1 to 10 percent. When I say this, people think I'm pulling their leg, but I assure them I'm serious. Then I explain that motivation is something we learn. Yes, some people seem to be born highly motivated. They are always buzzing about, soaking up everything the world has to offer, founding businesses and forging ahead. But most people need to nurture motivation like a precious resource, laying the groundwork for it to flourish and establishing processes to care and feed it through the routine ins and outs of daily life.

Proper motivation rests on what I call the three irrefutable laws of motivation, which are (1) make it fun, (2) avoid pain, and (3) improve. These laws were so important to Chris's success that I am giving them their own chapter and hoping my examples will inspire readers to use what I have learned to develop their own achievement habits.

◆ **12** ◆

FUN, PAINLESS, AND HABIT-FORMING
The Good Life

The three irrefutable laws of motivation—having fun, avoiding pain, and improving every day—may sound easy, but if they were easy, more people would practice them rather than submit to the grueling on-and-off relationships they usually have with exercise, diet, and other programs. The truth is, the 1% Better method takes discipline and perseverance. Above all, it requires patience, a virtue often in short supply in today's world.

As described in the preceding chapter, 1% Better is an achievement habit. With Chris, our first objective was to create this habit, which we knew would take a long time. We were not looking for short-term gains; we were looking to create lifelong habits. Our first battle was working long enough to make sure 1% Better became a mindset habit for Chris. Only then could we move to the next phase of sustained growth. Developing this mindset habit took the better part of a year, and sustaining it took another six months.

When strengthening Chris's core became a priority, we set up a progression of push-ups, sit-ups, and squats that advanced him, day to day, from doing a single one of each exercise to four sets of fifty, or two hundred each, in the lead-up to IRONMAN Florida. We did the same thing with biking, running, and swimming. Just one more until one day he was competing in a 140.6-mile triathlon.

HAVING FUN. While we were doing all of this training, we built a consistent element of fun into every workout. Fun makes building habits easier. If it is not fun, you are more likely to stop doing it. Chris is a social creature, so whenever possible I included other people besides me in his workouts. Chris may not have been excited about going out and doing a 100-mile bike ride, but if he had ten people doing it with him and he was included in the friendly banter of athletes on a long training run, it was a whole different experience. Community is a critical element in making a habit fun. For Chris, being part of a community connects to his dream of being like everybody else. It's constant reinforcement of being included, which we further reinforced with a group brunch at Waffle House.

All of us have something we enjoy doing that brings us pleasure. The key to making 1% Better work is to build that pleasure into your process of improvement. Far from denying it or suppressing it, you should consider leveraging that pleasure as a motivator that pushes you to reach your goal. The pleasure will not undermine the goal but will actually serve the goal. To return to our weight-loss example, cutting out a nightly beer or glass of wine would certainly reduce your calorie count, but would it improve your quality of life? Or would cutting out that drink deprive you of something you look forward to after a workout or hard day's work and make accomplishing those things a little bit harder?

Chris especially liked hanging out with Simone. The two of them often met to do workouts together, including running, biking, swimming, and strength training. But she made it fun by routinely posting selfies of herself and Chris after each workout. In these photos, Chris could see wonderful moments in his life taking place over and over again in the company of others. One day there would be a photo of a group of Special Olympics triathletes posing with Simone and Hector after a 9-mile bike ride. Another day's photo would feature Chris and Simone after a workout or event. Chris was becoming a proficient reader and enjoyed reading Simone's upbeat postings, which often praised him for his positivity and showcased her love of him. This one, posted on Facebook on August 12, 2019, was typical: "Saturday's race was difficult, hot, and miserable, but this is why I'm going to keep trying despite better judgment: I love this kid with all my heart. He is kind, generous, silly, and the most positive person you'll ever meet. He and his family are an incredible source of happiness, love, and positivity."

As I've said, like most of us, Chris loves to eat. He has his favorite foods that he prefers to enjoy in certain ways. For example, nothing helped Chris get through a long run or bike ride like knowing that an ice cream cone or sundae awaited him at the end. He could also be motivated by knowing that ahead of him was an evening curled up on the couch with popcorn, a Sprite, and a favorite movie. I did whatever I had to do to associate his daily habits with fun. People told me that he shouldn't eat junk food. I believe that one person's junk food is another's vital fuel. How vital was fun to Chris's development? During our weekly planning sessions, when Chris and I would go over the previous week's progress and plan the next week, we also talked about how we would reward each new personal best.

"If I get a personal best this week, can we go to P.F. Chang's?" he asked. "Can I have a Sprite with my meal?" I always said yes.

This way of motivating Chris did not sit well with his other coaches. They were wedded to a more traditional strategy that served them and the people they generally worked with: highly self-motivated people who could and would do anything their coach asked of them, an admittedly small percentage of us and not one that included Chris. Many athletes become addicted to endurance sports for how they make them feel. The surge of endorphins puts them in a cherished zone. I'm sure Chris gets some enjoyment from this as well, but I seriously doubt Chris could have gone 1 mile, let alone 140 miles, without the constant motivation of fun, friends, and food along the way.

The 1% Better mindset is a celebration of life, not a grind.

AVOIDING PAIN. If there is a main obstacle to long-term improvement, it is pain.

Pain is the highest hurdle to overcome, and when the mental pain gets too hard to bear, people just quit. Our minds will do anything to maximize pleasure and avoid pain. If you approach training from a no pain, no gain perspective, however, you will try to push yourself to, and through, the level of pain where you ought to pull back. You will push yourself to a point where you feel pain for several days afterward. You will then need time to recover. The problem with recovery times of three, four, five, or more days is that they pit our brains against our bodies. The pain gets embedded in the brain. Even six months later the pain still feels like it did when you were first injured. The brain will continue to convince you not to do whatever you did to hurt yourself ever again. With Chris, I tried to ensure that we avoided these kinds of residual pain, with their long recovery times, at all costs. Instead, we focused on small improvements.

Everyone has a mental breaking point. It takes hold of us much earlier than the physical breaking point because the body has a much higher pain threshold than the brain. The trick is to teach the brain not to quit.

I found that the easiest way to do this with Chris was to divide pain into categories of "real" and "fake." The real pain was what he felt when he crashed his bike and had to get stitches. The real pain took time to go away. In contrast to real pain, fake pain was what Chris felt when his lungs, heart, or legs were working beyond a level of comfort and his brain registered that as pain.

It wasn't *actually* fake—Chris did feel something when his legs or lungs burned—but the pain was something that he could quickly overcome. We had to help him understand how it differed from the pain that truly debilitated him. I heavily used the word *fake* to do this. This pain was fake because it went away as soon as Chris stopped. One proven method for teaching this is with a tub of cold water. When you first step into the tub, the rush of blood away from your legs to protect your vital organs makes it feel as though you are being bombarded by a thousand small needles. This is excruciating—but it is also fake pain.

When I had Chris spend ten seconds in a forty-eight-degree tub and then jump into a hot tub, he immediately felt much better. The next day he spent eleven seconds in the cold tub before getting into a hot tub. Each day he did 1 percent more. A couple of weeks later, he could sit in the cold tub for two minutes. At this stage, something amazing happened: it stopped hurting. The brain got used to the pain, and it went away. Chris started to enjoy being in the cold tubs, and he reaped the additional benefit of reducing swelling after training. Eventually Chris fell in love with the cold tub. Sitting in it is now one of his favorite things to do at the end of a workout in the gym.

Something similar happened with running. Chris hated running, so we started by running slowly for a mile. If he experienced too much pain, he would slow down to walk and let the pain go away, then start running again. As we approached the last minute, he and I would race, cranking the speed up higher. He loves to race and win, so that last minute was yet another moment of fun, one he always looked forward to. But it was also teaching him to convert the fake pain into something fun. Eventually he got to where he could run a mile at a very slow pace and still finish the last minute fast. The pain hurt less as he got in better shape, and his brain got stronger as we increased the speed and the distance.

IMPROVING EVERY DAY. The process of converting something painful into something pleasurable brings us to the last immutable law for forming habits. 1% Better is an achievement habit. It is a mindset. An achievement habit takes hold when you do ten push-ups during today's workout, and the next time you go into it knowing you will do eleven push-ups. There might be one day or three days between workouts—it doesn't matter—but the achievement habit instructs you to do one more, and that is what you do.

Here's how the achievement habit worked with Chris. Since he disliked running, let's look at that. We started running for one minute as fast as he could. As the pain reached its peak at the end of the minute, we slowed down to walk for two minutes, and his pain would go away. Eventually we built up to two minutes of running and feeling some pain, followed by two minutes of walking. We increased the ratio of running to walking to six minutes of running and one minute of walking. Then we switched to running a mile and walking for one minute. Over time Chris increased his run speed and kept the walking time of one minute a constant. Eventually he got to where he could run six minutes and walk one minute fast enough to complete a marathon running portion at the end of an IRONMAN triathlon. We used a similar progression of high intensity and low intensity for the bike and swim portions.

Not only did this gradual improvement make Chris's pain temporary and easy to handle, but it also provided a regular rush of endorphins. Think about it. If you master doing ten push-ups, you will soon reach the point where doing them fails to give a surge to your brain. If you do 1 percent better each time, you will receive a regular boost of endorphins. On the other hand, if you focus on making huge breakthroughs that require long recovery times, you will experience far fewer bounces of pleasure.

Imagine two different approaches to accomplishing something. The first approach involves a commitment to no pain, no gain. This approach includes a lot of intense, furious, painful, injury-riddled exercise that gets you results fast. But for 99 percent of us, this is unsustainable, and we will quit. For 1 percent of the population, this approach will work, and they will go from average to great in about three months. So if you want immediate results and you have what it takes to push yourself, this is the approach for you—provided you are one of that 1 percent.

Chris's approach was easy, painless, injury-free, fun, and habit-forming. Of course, it took a long time to get some results. If you take this path to trying to improve yourself, there is a 50 percent chance of completing the program and being successful. That may not sound grand, but it is a 5,000 percent higher success rate than the first approach! It may take you as long as a year to see the same results as the first approach, but you will develop a lifestyle habit, a mental habit, a mindset. You will enjoy it as it becomes more permanent. And you will have an amazing foundation for continuous growth.

I often tell people that the 1% Better concept is profoundly counterintuitive. When they ask what I mean, I say that people who fail at the 1% Better method don't fail because it is too difficult. *They fail because it is too easy.* People are so accustomed to hearing that they need to outwork everyone to succeed that they cannot discipline themselves to slow down. For example, doing 1 percent better for a month or so, people may start to feel very good and decide they are ready to ramp up things a bit and progress faster. So if they were doing ten push-ups one day and saw all the crazy people carrying on at the gym, they might think, *Ten push-ups are too easy. Tomorrow I'll forge new ground and do twenty-five push-ups!*

The next time they do push-ups, they will do twenty-five and feel as if they're on top of the world. They will think that 1 percent better was holding them back—that they are part of that top group of overachievers! Usually this marks the beginning of the end for them because now their chest will be very sore for five days. Then they will not do any more push-ups for at least five days. Their habit had been to improve 1 percent every two days with no pain. Now it is replaced by being in pain for five days before they can exercise again. When they resume exercise, will they keep increasing their workload? Few can do this over an extended period. The more likely scenario will be that they reduce their workload.

Even if you decide to do more push-ups, perhaps twelve to get back on track, you are not 1 percent better. You are 500 percent worse. And your mind hates 500 percent worse. You just sabotaged your success. The best case is that you just lost momentum because you have to rebuild your mind back to feeling good about trying to be 1 percent better. This is what I mean by suggesting the 1% Better approach is too easy for many people to master. It takes patience. Like the vast majority of us, Chris would not have lasted a week trying to power his way through his workouts in the typical no pain, no gain fashion. The good news was that he never had to.

A triathlon or even an IRONMAN triathlon is a great vehicle for applying consistent improvement because you can shift from one event to the other, keeping things interesting and varied. Chris did not have to improve in all three disciplines every week. Some weeks emphasized running while others focused on biking or swimming. The keys were being able to look back at each week and pinpoint where he improved, then look ahead to the coming week to decide on his improvement goals for the days ahead. We were able to make each step forward into a habit of achievement. And we always reminded Chris of his dreams.

For more than a year, as training got more intense, we taught Chris's brain to recognize and deal with the fake pain. That's why Chris never quit. We spent two years helping him build a mindset.

As he says, "My dream is bigger than the fake pain."

THE ACHIEVEMENT-HABIT MINDSET

This book was written not only to chronicle and celebrate Chris's achievements but also to offer the 99 percent of us—who react better to 1 percent improvements instead of the no pain, no gain mindset—some tips and tools for rewriting their own narratives. A quote widely attributed to Aristotle says, "We are what we repeatedly do. Excellence, therefore, is not an act, but a habit." The 1% Better concept is not a formula. It is a personal commitment to developing achievement habits and a mindset of continuous improvement. These are not habits practiced by the superachievers. I hope never to read another story about a billionaire who attributes his success to the feeling of accomplishment he gets from making his bed every morning. Achievement habits work by connecting our conscious goals with our subconscious need for pleasure, community, self-esteem, material comfort, and so forth. As we all know, new habits are hard to form, and old habits are even harder to change.

My favorite book on developing habits is *Mini Habits: Smaller Habits, Bigger Results* by Stephen Guise. I have gleaned from this book some concepts that explain why habits are so hard to form:

- It takes an average of sixty-six days to form a habit.
- The brain is wired to protect you against big changes and will sabotage your efforts.
- Habits are like muscles; once you've developed a habit, you can make it stronger.
- Trying to develop more than one to two new habits simultaneously will lead to failure.[9]

I told Chris that if he wanted to reach his dreams, he just needed to keep getting 1 percent better and eat more to fuel his increased activity. Of course, Chris's face lit up when I talked about eating more. If there's one thing Chris likes about eating, it's *eating more.*

He said, "Okay, Dad, let's do it," but then he paused. "Dad, but why should I do it?"

I said that's a great question, and I figured since God gave Chris the vision to be a world champ, I also assumed He gave Chris a dream big enough to achieve it.

Your unconscious and conscious mind carry on a continuous dialogue. Therefore, you have to be deliberate about feeding and protecting your unconscious mind against conscious things that could undermine it. For example, from the moment Chris used the phrase "smoky-hot blond," he (and mostly I) drew a great deal of criticism from just about every important woman in Chris's life, including my mom, Patty, and Jacky. I asked them why. The typical answer was it is disrespectful, and they were worried what others might think. I resisted any effort to get Chris to drop the expression because it was his dream in his words. I believe someone's dreams are the single most important factor in their success. Also remember, this was on his dream board in his room with all his goals and plans. To change it, I would have had to cross it out and replace his words with my words. I didn't want to mess around with his dream. I believe that Chris's language to express his dream is the glue that holds it together in his mind. Should we—could we—replace "smoky-hot blond" with a politically correct answer? Would these words be Chris's words? Would he understand them the same way? This is a high-wire act we are on, and I am not willing to tamper with the technique halfway across the rope.

Eventually we helped Chris add some words to soften the phrase. Now he says a "smoky-hot blond wife from Minnesota, *like my mom.*"

Changing Chris's words would change his dream and possibly undermine it. Changing the language he uses to talk about training would have a similar effect. For example, he wanted to run ten miles because he thought it was a cool thing to do, and his friends were doing it and having fun along the way. As far as the IRONMAN triathlon went, he wanted to do it exactly as fast as needed to complete the event on time—seventeen hours, not the twelve hours or less the elite athletes were hoping to attain.

In a strange and counterintuitive way, my challenge was to protect Chris not only from the naysayers but also from the overachievers who thought he could progress much faster than we planned.

"Look, you guys," I said to the overachievers. "You can't say stuff like that. You can't start painting this picture of all these things you think he could do; he's not motivated to do them. He doesn't even like running. He doesn't want to break any time limits or congratulate himself for eating only the healthiest foods. He wants to run, have fun, and then go home and eat a big bowl of ice cream while watching *Chicago P.D.*"

◆ ◆ ◆

People who have read articles about Chris or seen him interviewed on TV have asked me whether we applied the 1% Better concept literally with him. They also have asked whether I recommend that others apply the concept literally. The answer is no to both questions. The concept is not a formula, although anybody could be forgiven for thinking it is. The 1% Better mindset is a guideline for steady progress. To be successful in applying it, you have to be patient. With Chris, we did not obsess about the literalness of 1 percent, but we did obsess about the assumptions we made about progress. Let me show you what I mean.

If I wasn't patient with measuring Chris's improvement, I would have missed something very important. When he began with Special Olympics, he was not able to compete right away with the other athletes. The majority of them had autism or other intellectual disabilities. Physically, however, they were more in line with typical athletes. Down syndrome affects Chris both physically and intellectually, so he spent the first nine or ten months of the Special Olympics triathlon competitions coming in last place. It was hard to watch my son come in last all the time. Chris wasn't enthralled with it either. People with Down syndrome compare themselves to other people just like you and I do. But we stuck with our program, and Chris gradually kept getting better and better.

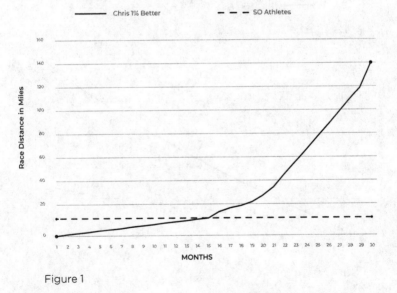

Chris vs. Other Elite Special Olympics Athletes
(Triathlon Distance in Miles Completed over 30 Months)

Figure 1

I have created a couple of graphs to offer some visualization of Chris's progress over time. Figure 1 compares Chris's progress with that of the other triathletes over thirty months participating in Special Olympics. Notice how far ahead of Chris they are between the first and tenth months. Chris's improvement was steady even though he lagged well behind the other athletes. Remember, in what we may characterize in more human, experiential terms, this line on the graph meant many last-place finishes for Chris.

Notice how between months ten and fifteen Chris began to close the gap with his fellow athletes ever so slightly. It's barely perceptible, but it is consistent. After that, the performance shift never loses ground.

Chris vs. Other Elite Special Olympics Athletes
(Improvement Percentage in Time for Finishing a 15-Mile Sprint)

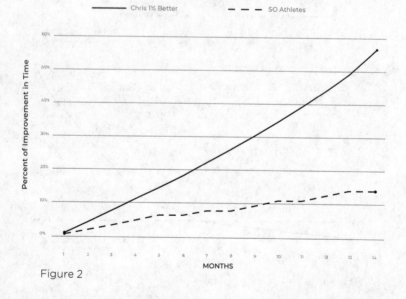

Figure 2

Note how in the fifteenth month Chris caught up with his peers, and a month later he surpassed them for the first time. From that point on, his progress improved exponentially. Also take a look at Figure 2. What you are seeing in this remarkable trajectory is the positive impact of momentum: a compounding effect that kicked in and lifted the ceiling of how much Chris could improve. This is the 1% Better mindset.

The problem we had was that the acceleration didn't kick in for about eighteen months. Most parents and coaches would never have the patience to stick with it that long. I didn't either—at least not at first. I had no idea this acceleration was going to happen. When it did, and I began to see the gap closing, disappearing, and then reversing dramatically, I felt encouraged. I had a Billy Beane moment when the quality of Chris's small improvements added up to superior performance.

In that line I traced on a simple graph was vindication for an approach that had worked well enough in measuring progress with salespeople but had, until then, been unproven by me in other applications. From beginning to end, improving Chris's performance took thirty months. Almost all of the major growth took place between months twenty and thirty.

When Chris was doing sprint triathlons and thinking about doing an Olympic triathlon, everybody thought it was too much. Once he did the Olympic triathlon and we talked of doing an IRONMAN 70.3 race, everyone repeated the chorus. Then Chris made the jump to the ultra distance only six months after the half distance because we had spent the previous year laying the groundwork, giving him the mental discipline required to form an achievement habit that could take him to the next level.

◆ ◆ ◆

If you move too fast, your body hits a wall before you have the chance to develop the 1% Better achievement habit. You need about nine months of steady progress to build the habit. It's important to differentiate that, unlike most habits that involve physical behaviors, this is a mental achievement habit. This is why I keep referring to it as the 1% Better mindset. If you do try to progress too quickly, your body will stop improving before you have had time to build a mental habit. Remember, the plan is first about building the mind and, second, about building the body. The body will catch up eventually, but first you must build the mind.

Look at Figure 2 again and notice how the other Special Olympics athletes in the sprint saw improvements, including some fairly dramatic ones. After this, however, their progress started to flatline. This flatlining effect is precisely what happens to most of us who pursue an improvement plan that emphasizes the big breakthroughs at the expense of smaller improvements.

Think about it: most of the diet and exercise plans people try end up not working for them. Why do we keep doing the same things? Einstein is often credited with having said that the clinical definition of insanity is doing the same thing over and over again and expecting different results. Maybe it is time to try something else, something that is counterintuitive and goes against the grain of what you thought you were supposed to do. Something that will give you modest results early on but not to the magnitude promised elsewhere. The 1% Better plan is designed to provide long-term success and to do it painlessly. Most plans focus on getting you to the final result as quickly as possible; the 1% Better plan focuses on building your mind through a process. It is less concerned with a final result because your improvement never ends. As I said, it is counterintuitive.

Here is an example of this idea in action. As Chris looked forward to the IRONMAN World Championship in Hawaii on October 9, 2021, his biggest challenge was probably biking 19 miles uphill in one direction and 19 miles downhill in the other direction. He needed to average 14 miles an hour across the entire race. Most athletes will labor at between 5 and 8 miles an hour on the ascent and make up the lost time by going 30 or 40 miles an hour on the descent. Chris could not control the bike at that speed, which meant we needed to increase his uphill speed—by more than most people need to—while helping him increase his downhill speed to about 20 miles an hour, without him feeling panicked or uncontrolled.

After taking some time off, we had only eight months to prepare for the Hawaii event, so our timeline was compressed. The first thing we did was find a place to train. We live near Sugarloaf Mountain, which is slightly more elevated than the terrain in the Hawaii race. Our goal for the first thirty days was to make Chris feel in complete control and believe he could get up and down the hill. If he believed it, his body would also believe it. On his first try, he got about halfway up the hill, rested for a bit, and finished the second half. We did this twice a week. On the downhill segment, we taught him to steadily and methodically apply brake pressure so that he controlled his speed at all times, and to keep pedaling at all times because pedaling is what allows you to balance the bike in Hawaii's strong crosswinds. The last thing you want to do is coast downhill against strong crosswinds!

In that first week we got Chris going 6 miles an hour downhill and in complete control.

The next time we went to Sugarloaf, Chris made it all the way up at about 5 miles an hour without resting, and on the descent, he increased his speed from 6 to 8 miles an hour—1 percent better—and maintained complete control. The following week we increased the sets and upped the descent speed to 10 miles an hour. The key to making this work was planning backward from the October 9 race date to determine a training schedule that would gradually and comfortably allow him to increase his speed to where he could go 10 miles an hour uphill and 20 downhill and feel in control the whole way.

When I speak with people about 1% Better, I often hear words and phrases such as "can't," "too hard," "impossible," or "takes too much time." I tell my listeners to imagine something. One day they are running a single lap around a track. Soon they run a lap and a quarter, then a lap and a half. Some time goes by, and they proudly celebrate their first mile run. Sometimes they don't feel like running, but after they do, they feel like a million bucks. Since they like feeling that way, they keep on increasing their mileage, slowly and steadily. And then, two years later, they find themselves running a marathon or half triathlon.

That's how I motivated a twenty-year-old with Down syndrome to do an IRONMAN triathlon. One of the greatest joys of my life has been being by my son's side, helping him to pursue his dreams. In two and a half years, Chris has grown from an eighteen-year-old with Down syndrome to an athlete completing an IRONMAN race and now preparing to compete with the world's greatest triathletes in the IRONMAN World Championship in Kona, Hawaii. He has become a highly coveted motivational speaker and the coauthor of this book. Doing the full distance is amazing, but an individual with Down syndrome doing public speaking is even more remarkable. Chris has stepped up to the challenge and can now deliver a twenty-minute speech from memory in front of a thousand people. All this happened in the last two years by getting 1 percent better.

According to a study published in the *European Journal of Social Psychology* titled "How Are Habits Formed," it takes around sixty-six days to form what I call a "behavior habit."[10] An achievement habit takes nine to twelve months. It has to be built slowly, but once you have that foundation, you have it forever.

Achievement habits differ from behavioral habits because they are about the mind not the body. For example, many people who go to the gym go three to four to five times a week as part of their routines. At the gym they go through a predictable set of exercises that they will sometimes switch up in the name of keeping things interesting and varied. Maybe one day it's a Zumba class, and the next day it's a treadmill run followed by some strength training with weights. These folks are in good shape because they have maintained a behavior habit. They are significantly fitter (and better off) than those who don't go to the gym. The majority of these people will be in roughly the same shape in January as they are the following December. Their habit is one of exercise, and for many people this seems enough.

An achievement habit is for somebody who has a different purpose, which is to improve. And improvement is a mental habit more than it is a physical habit. Those who go to the gym for the purpose of improvement are not trying to "get in a workout" but to make themselves a little better. One year after joining a gym, while the person with a behavior habit continues to do twenty or thirty push-ups at each session, the person with an achievement habit like Chris will go from doing one to two hundred push-ups. And you know what? It won't be hard. One of the major benefits of this kind of habit is that it not only makes you fitter and healthier physically but also makes you stronger mentally because you have built a mindset that can handle more and more and more.

What is more, an achievement habit is like a muscle that you use to develop other skills. You can go from push-ups to swimming, golf, playing the piano, speaking French, or baking French bread because you have rewired your brain. The mind is so strong that once you have rewired it, you can take the body wherever you want to go.[11]

Another counterintuitive facet of 1% Better is that failure is the secret to success. Winning makes you feel good, but losing teaches you more. Failure can either deflate you or energize you to come back stronger. When you choose to do the latter and succeed, that is the best feeling of all. The best addiction in life is achievement. When you get hooked on achievement, it becomes a habit. It's something you think about every day. All kinds of incredible opportunities will become available to you. It is like a game in which each week you open up a new level and new possibilities become available to you that you never even imagined. When you develop a 1% Better achievement mindset, your brain acts like a magnet and attracts anything that helps it feed the habit. So you get hooked on achievement.

In June 2019 Chris gave his first motivational speech. I had been doing some sales training for a client, and I asked my contact at the company whether Chris could speak for five minutes to the one thousand salespeople who were attending my workshop in Orlando. After I explained that I used the same foundation of steady, 1% Better improvement to help Chris become a triathlete that I used to train salespeople, my contact agreed to have him speak. Chris delivered the speech well and focused on how our 1% Better method enabled him to become a triathlete.

Will he have a career in motivational speaking? That is hard to know long term, but in the first three months of 2021, Chris had done over twenty virtual speeches for thousands of people who work in companies such as Microsoft, Walmart, Dell, Skillsoft, and Check Point, and momentum seemed to be building as word spread about his inspirational speeches. We have hired coaches who are helping us identify the top thousand or so words that people use in conversation. Chris is learning the meaning of the words and their pronunciations so he can use them in public settings. We will apply the 1% Better approach here as well. For example, we will patiently and steadily go through the first thousand words. We will add to these over time but never so fast that Chris is unable to learn them well enough to be able to understand what each word means, how he can use it in a sentence and a conversation, and how he can pronounce it clearly enough to be understood. These are all measurable metrics and help make him a better speaker, which includes handling interviews—because he's going to be interviewed a lot.

One thing is for sure: if Chris can go from being a Special Olympics sprint triathlete to an IRONMAN finisher in just over a year, I would be the last person to put a lid on what he can accomplish as a motivational speaker.

◆ ◆ ◆

As the son of immigrant parents, I grew up believing that America was the land of hope and opportunity. Your future wasn't something that was given to you. You had to earn it. And even if the playing field wasn't always even, if you worked hard and held yourself accountable, you could change your life's trajectory and that of your family's forever.

Since this American dream was part of my DNA, I always believed Chris could aspire to greater things if we did our part to push him in the right direction. But all of the pushing in the world would not have succeeded in moving Chris across that finish line if he hadn't had it in himself to do it.

None of us are born to undertake an IRONMAN triathlon. It is a great endeavor, like writing a novel or building a bridge or starting a successful company, that takes courage and stamina and imagination. Not everybody is cut out for such undertakings. But who would have thought Chris was one of the people who is? When I think about that, I better understand why complete strangers came up to him to hug him and me that day in Panama City Beach. Some were fellow athletes, while others were family members or friends of people with Down syndrome who had heard about Chris and drove more than ten hours to witness this previously unthinkable feat and thank him personally for changing the narrative about what is possible for this incredible group of people.

There are a lot of you out there—I know, because many of you have written to Chris or to me to thank him for inspiring you to believe in your family member, friend, or yourself. If you are able to look beyond your immediate horizons to pursue your dreams, like Chris did, you have already taken a first step toward accomplishing this yourself.

14

NOW IT'S YOUR TURN

You're probably reading this book because you read about or saw television news coverage on my son, Chris, and his historical achievement of becoming the first person with Down syndrome to complete an IRONMAN triathlon. Chris's story inspired you, and you hoped that the book would give you some behind-the-scenes context to help you better understand how Chris managed to accomplish this remarkable feat. I hope you have not been disappointed by the book in this regard.

In large part we wanted to celebrate the story of Chris's accomplishment, as well as record a history of a father and son's adventure together into uncharted territory, a journey made by our entire family and a close network of friends you've read about in these pages.

But the book was written for another reason as well. I

wanted to inspire others to question the limits they have placed on themselves or that institutions around them, where they worked, went to school, or recreated, have placed on them. I wanted to inspire others to change their lives in ways large or small. But if I was going to try to do this, I felt I needed to do more than simply inspire. I also needed to offer a means and method to help others develop a 1% Better habit for themselves. To be sure, if you read the main narrative of this carefully, you will be able to acquire a great many tips and examples to follow. But I wanted to provide a focused, step-by-step, practical guide to practicing the 1% Better method.

That is why I decided to include an appendix. I encourage you to use any part of, or all of, the appendix as a template for your 1% Better project. As you'll see, you don't have to aspire to do an IRONMAN triathlon to get a lifetime of value from devoting yourself to gradual improvement. Of course, you could still work on getting better at things without the use of the 1% Better method. I would never claim to have created the one and only means of getting better at doing something! But I would say that 1% Better has worked for Chris in spectacular enough fashion to offer some useful tools for you to use.

So go ahead. Give it a try. Pick something that you've always wanted to do or to be better at—something that would improve your fitness, increase your bank account, help you acquire a new skill, or pursue an interest more deeply than you've managed so far. One of the problems most of us have in making a change in our lives is that we haven't really thought about what we want to accomplish in sufficient detail. "I want to learn how to play tennis" is too vague and open-ended to motivate most people. But what if your dream was to enjoy the health and social benefits of becoming a proficient adult tennis player? Now, there's something you could sink your teeth into. You may even know people who regularly play Saturday afternoon doubles matches that you could participate in if only you could play!

Another trip wire to improvement is not knowing how to monitor our progress or what success looks like when we see it. You'll find guidelines for all of these key aspects of self-improvement in the appendix. In keeping with our example of tennis, you might begin by taking a single lesson through a public recreation department and hitting balls with a partner once a week for half an hour. From there you might take another lesson and from there progress to a package of six lessons and twice-a-week playing with a partner. Before very long, you might reach a milestone of becoming too good for your partner and have to seek out better players—but not too good! You'll be prepared for this next milestone because your lessons and growing confidence will introduce you to more players.

If you really care about becoming a tennis player, you'll want to feel rested and energized when you play, so you'll begin eating better and getting more sleep, which will make you feel even better and more satisfied with your tennis habit. And you'll know you've accomplished your dream when you find yourself joining that foursome for a game of mixed doubles. But enough of my yakking! Now it's your turn: go out there and get 1 percent better!

ACKNOWLEDGMENTS

Completing an IRONMAN® triathlon is an extraordinary accomplishment for anybody, and for Chris it was, well, a historic event. Writing about our adventure was also an adventure in itself and, much like preparing to participate in an IRONMAN race, one that could not have been completed without the support of others. Between running my own company and working with Team Chris on a daily basis, I found myself sorely pressed for writing time. I'm proud to say that I was able to lean pretty heavily on some exceptional talent, especially my cowriter, *New York Times* bestselling author Don Yaeger and his editing partner Dave Moore. I am especially grateful for Don's suggestion that we delve into a bit of Nikic family history as a way of furnishing some context for understanding Chris's drive.

Starting closest to home, Chris's mom (and my wife), Patty, helped with the sections of the book that deal with Down syndrome and the imposing physical and mental challenges it can have on a newborn and a young person growing up. She offered a window into the social and educational challenges of living with Down syndrome, especially as they relate to school placement, and she continues to humble me with her selfless devotion to Chris during his formative years and today. Patty's personal memories give a peek into the living heart of the Nikic household, and I certainly hope you realize Chris couldn't have a better mama bear looking out for him!

We would never have been able to make Chris's personality and charisma come to life without the insights offered by his sister, Jacky, and friend and Unified partner Simone Goodfriend, who naturally had different relationships with Chris than I did. I tried to include as many of their wonderful anecdotes and as much of their wisdom as I could in this book. Thanks to their stories, we have a more well-rounded picture of Chris than we would have had I alone described his life and accomplishments! Not the least of these anecdotes came from the many Facebook posts Simone shared with me detailing the exuberance of her and Chris's relationship, training sessions, and the larger community of athletes who welcomed Chris into their ranks.

As the big sister, Jacky always had her baby brother's back, but this never stopped her from also having Chris's number like nobody else alive, so my recounting of the humorous side of the Nikic household is owed much to her sense of humor.

Chris also had his angels who played pivotal roles in his journey and growth as an IRONMAN athlete. This group includes Hector Torres, who trained Chris and helped develop our training plans that I aligned to Chris's unique strengths. Leo Briceno, who helped with ocean swims to get Chris ready to tackle his biggest obstacle. Carlos Mendoza and Jennifer

Sturgess, who trained with Chris, especially on those long and grueling weekends, as well as assisted Chris as guiders during the IRONMAN race.

To Chris's Unified partner and guardian angel, Dan Grieb, I owe a mountain-sized debt for his vivid descriptions of competing in the IRONMAN triathlon. Dan's willingness to be open about his own background and motivation to pursue triathlons added an emotional ballast to understanding his extraordinary work with Chris.

We started writing this book just as the world was catching on to Chris's story, so I benefited from reading other published accounts of Chris's development and historic race. While nobody other than Chris and Dan was closer to the action than I was, I benefited from the storytelling talent of Kurt Streeter in his impassioned *New York Times* account of the major ups and downs that followed Chris and Dan every step of the way in Panama City Beach. Tom Couch's *Special Fathers Network* gave me the chance not only to do some digging through key details of the Nikic family history when we appeared on its *Dad to Dad* podcast with David Hirsch but also to immerse myself into the world of triathlons. And Parveen Panwar's interview with Chris, Dan, and me for *Authority Magazine* helped me think through and articulate the ways we applied the 1% Better method to Chris's training and development.

And speaking of the 1% Better concept, in writing a book about the advantages of making small changes over time rather than one or two heroic pivots, I would like to give a special shout out to several people: Michael Lewis, author of *Moneyball: The Art of Winning an Unfair Game*; James

Clear, author of the bestselling book *Atomic Habits: An Easy and Proven Way to Build Good Habits and Break Bad Ones*; Stephen Guise, author of *Mini Habits: Smaller Habits, Bigger Results*; and Phillippa Lally et al., who published the 2009 article "How Are Habits Formed: Modeling Habit Formation in the Real World" in the *European Journal of Social Psychology*. All were indispensable for turning complex ideas into the story of Chris's step-by-step journey from couch potato to IRONMAN athlete.

The late, great coach John Wooden may not have been alive in body to help me write this book, but his words and humble spirit of discipline and improvement guided this project every step of the way. Thank you, Coach.

I wish to thank Special Olympics and Special Olympics Florida for sharing important information about how their programs work, how they are staffed, and how the organization established its Global Ambassador's Program, of which Chris is now a Champion Ambassador, to extend its mission worldwide. It is impossible to write about this organization and the dedicated and loving volunteers it attracts to its orbit without being eternally grateful that it exists to extend the boundaries of what is deemed possible for millions of athletes around the world. Specifically, I want to thank Wynne McFarland, who started the Special Olympics triathlon program in Florida, and Sherry Wheelock, who made it happen.

My understanding of the history and growth of the IRONMAN triathlon, from its humble beginnings in Honolulu to its current stature as one of the world's iconic competitions, was gleaned from the IRONMAN Group's own

"The IRONMAN Story." The IRONMAN Group webpage also contains detailed descriptions, photographs, and maps showing the swimming, cycling, and running courses comprising the Panama City Beach event. These refreshed my memory of the actual event and furnished the geographical particulars on which I could build an exciting narrative of Chris's journey through 140.6-miles of sunlit and moonlit waters and streets.

I am grateful to the producers of the Worldometer website (www.worldometers.info) for providing population statistics that enabled me to put Chris's achievement in a quantitative as well as qualitative perspective. And ditto for Russell Cox and his excellent website, CoachCox.co.uk, which furnished much-needed, year-by-year data on IRONMAN event participation statistics.

My lifelong appreciation of Roger Bannister's historic sub-four-minute mile came from Roger Bannister's *The Four-Minute Mile* and, more recently, "Sir Roger Bannister" on the Academy of Achievement website.

Finally, a big shout-out to the editorial team at W Publishing Group—Damon Reiss, Kyle Olund, Paula Major, and others—for believing in the project from the start and keeping us on a writing and review schedule that would ensure the book's publication in advance of the 2021 IRONMAN World Championship in Hawaii, in which Chris is entered to compete as an athlete. Damon, Kyle, and Paula's appreciative insights into our approach to telling Chris's story buoyed us during the editing process, and their astute reading of the chapters made each and every one of them, and the whole book, much better.

APPENDIX
The 1% Better System

Through Chris's story we hope to offer you a more effective approach to achieving your important goals and dreams by using a different system that is better aligned to use your strengths and overcome obstacles. We all are born with certain strengths and weaknesses, and our successes, in large part, owe much to how those strengths and weaknesses align with a success system designed by American society.

My parents brought me to the United States, and my strengths aligned well with this system. Had I stayed in Montenegro (in communism and poverty), I would be a different person, and I don't know how well my strengths would have fared. Over the past fifty years, I became familiar with and benefited from the American system. And now I am living the American dream, which includes seeing our son exert a positive impact on the world by challenging perceptions of what is possible.

Let me explain what I mean by "success system." Two

of the key parts to the system are education and sports. The system is designed to prepare children from the age of six to twenty-two to fit into socioeconomic brackets that define them for the rest of their lives. Of course there are exceptions, and individuals can make decisions later in life to change their socioeconomic status, but, for the most part, you can look at someone's progression through these years and predict where they are likely to end up.

Here is an oversimplified explanation of how this system works:

1. **EDUCATION.** Children are separated by grades and then subdivided into groups: gifted kids who attend advanced placement classes, a general pool of average-to-good students, and kids with special needs who are put in the corners to sit alone and be ignored (as was true for our son, Chris). Based on their grades and test scores, the top of the class ends up in the most prestigious universities (for example, our daughter, Jacky, who attended Dartmouth) or in the most successful programs at the colleges they attend. With rare exceptions, their paths are set for the rest of their lives.

2. **SPORTS.** Kids are separated as early as age six, and some are placed on travel teams in a particular sport so that by the time they are twelve years old or so, they are practically guaranteed to receive a college scholarship and have a shot at becoming a professional player. They are put in an environment to compete against the best, which in turn continues to separate them from the rest.

The premise of this book is to challenge that system, which is designed for people who are born with seemingly greater intelligence, ability, and drive, who are more likely to succeed in that system and, as a result, earn significantly higher wages and build greater wealth. This system is optimized for the top 1 percent and rapidly declines in effectiveness as it moves down to 5 percent, 10 percent, and so on. It's designed to accelerate the development of the top 10 percent and leave everyone else behind. Basically, as the following table shows, a very small part of the population succeeds while the rest fail.

Wages in the United States

2018 Annual Wages	
GROUP	WAGES (AVERAGE)
Top 1 percent of Earners	$737,697
Top 5 percent of Earners	$309,348
Top 10 percent of Earners	$158,002
Bottom 90 percent	$37,574

Source: Julia Kagan, "How Much Income Puts You in the Top 1%, 5%, 10%?" Investopedia, https://www.investopedia.com/personal-finance/how-much-income-puts-you-top-1-5-10/.

THE PROBLEM IS THE SYSTEM

I am a beneficiary of the current system because I was born with the intelligence, ability, and drive to succeed. The current system was designed for people like me. Our daughter, Jacky, is also gifted with the intelligence, ability, and drive to succeed in the current system. Raising her was easy: all my wife, Patty, and I had to do was guide her through the current system that was ideally suited to her abilities, which was simple enough since we had already successfully navigated through that system ourselves.

Chris, however, has special needs and lacks the intelligence, ability, and drive to succeed in the current system. Fortunately, God gave Patty and me the ability to recognize this problem and inspired us to take action to solve it. You see, our love for Chris is so great that we would turn the world upside down to help him succeed.

Chris gave us the inspiration to look deeper, and what we learned was simple: (1) Chris may not have the intelligence, ability, or drive to succeed in the current system, but (2) he has demonstrated the intelligence, ability, and drive to succeed through other means, so (3) we needed to design a different system that would focus on Chris's learning style, level of motivation, learning curve, intelligence, and abilities.

Chris spent the first eighteen years of his life in the American success system and ended up in the bottom 1 percent in practically every area of life. Then, from the ages of eighteen to twenty-one, Chris went through a new system—the 1% Better system—and made it to the top percentile in sports and income. Same person but different system and different results. Chris has learned what he can apply in his own life to reach his goals and dreams.

This appendix is about helping you to change the trajectory of your physical and financial future by helping you be the best you can be—1 percent better, one step at a time. You are not a failure. Your intelligence, ability, and drive may be better suited to a different system. The question is, are you willing to try a different system to change your future?

How We Did It

Using my engineering experience, I designed, built, and executed a system that was ideally suited to leverage Chris's unique strengths and overcome his weaknesses to go from the bottom 1 percent to the top 1 percent. His story can be your story too. Will this 1% Better system work for you? It's up to you, but a good place to start would be to consider the following:

1. If you keep doing the same thing, you'll keep getting the same thing.
2. As Franklin D. Roosevelt is widely attributed as saying, "Take a method and try it. If it fails, admit it frankly, and try another. But by all means, try something."

The beauty of the 1% Better system is that you will know in the first week if you have what it takes to succeed, and then every week after that you will validate it. Let me demonstrate by appealing to your sense of logic.

Here is a simple example using exercise: If you can walk 100 steps today, by getting 1 percent better, in one year you will be walking 3,700 steps. In two years, you will be walking up to 100,000 steps and should have no trouble walking a marathon. Imagine going from 100 steps to a marathon in two years. Do you think your life would change for the better if you could walk a marathon? Imagine your health, your energy, your attitude, and your confidence to achieve other things in your life.

But you don't have to wait to the end of one or two years to know if this is working for you. By the second day, you will be walking 101 steps. If you walk 100 steps today, do you have the ability and drive to walk 101 steps tomorrow? If you do, you'll have gotten 1 percent better. When you do it again and again, at the end of the first week you'll be up to 107—and you'll know that you have what it takes to do it for one week. Then do it again for one more week. Notice what is happening? Every week you will get stronger physically, and, more important, you will get stronger mentally. This is not about the body; this is about the mind. Success is mental. It is a 1% Better mindset. It is an achievement habit.

Contrary to what life has taught you up to this point, the last seven days just proved that you *do* have the intelligence, ability, and drive to succeed. When you do it again for three more weeks, you will prove that you have what it takes to succeed consistently for one month. What do you think that will do for your confidence? Now do it for two more months and you'll have proven you can do it for a quarter. Do that three more times and you'll have succeeded for a year. If you can do that, you will become a mental giant in comparison to where you were before. If you keep at it, the sky will truly be your limit.

1% BETTER MINDSET: BUILDING AN ACHIEVEMENT HABIT

Chris used the 1% Better system not only to complete an IRONMAN triathlon but also to launch a career that includes public speaking and business ownership. Remember, if you execute the 1% Better system in one area of your life for several years, you build a 1% Better mindset habit, and it spills over into every other area of your life. Chris offers living proof of that.

The 1% Better concept is not a formula; it is a personal commitment to developing achievement habits and a mindset of continuous improvement. Are you in?

Achievement habits work by connecting our conscious goals with our subconscious dreams and the need for pleasure, community, self-esteem, material comfort, and so forth. As we all know, new habits are hard to form, and old habits are even harder to change. Why the emphasis on the achievement habit? Because we have been trained on the value of behavior habits. Behaviors are physical. The achievement habit is mental. This habit is much more powerful because it engages your subconscious mind to look for solutions to obstacles. A habit happens automatically.

I mentioned in chapter 13 that my favorite book on developing habits is *Mini Habits: Smaller Habits, Bigger Results* by Stephen Guise. Guise offered some concepts to explain why habits are so hard to form. As a reminder, here is my restatement of those:

- It takes between 18 and 255 days to form a habit, with the average being 66 days.
- The brain is wired to protect you against big changes and will sabotage your efforts.
- Habits are like muscles; once you've developed a habit, you can make it stronger.

- Trying to develop more than one or two new habits simultaneously will lead to failure.[12]

Why is this important? Because your brain is like a battery. It starts each day fully charged—it has four bars. As with a battery, some activities drain the power faster than others. Behaviors that have not become habitual require much more energy than behaviors that are habits. When the brain is down to zero bars, it is done until you recharge it. So your brain's natural defense mechanism is to avoid adopting new behaviors that are not habits in order to preserve the brain's energy for thinking and emergencies. One way to maximize your brain's capacity is to identify habits that will help you achieve your most important goals and dreams.

If you can develop only one or two habits at one time, what is the best habit to hit your goals and dreams? I would argue that the best habit to develop is the 1% Better achievement habit itself!

THE THREE PRINCIPLES OF THE 1% BETTER SYSTEM

Principles are fundamental truths that serve as the foundation for a system of belief or behavior. An optimal system requires some key foundational principles that must be executed to produce the best results. The three critical underlying principles that drive the 1% Better system are the dream board, metrics, and coaching cadence.

Appendix

Principle #1: The Dream Board

The first principle necessary for implementing the 1% Better plan is to create a dream board, and it has five components:

1. The *dream* is the reason you do what you do and serves as the fuel to keep going when things get hard. Chris's dream was to make his own money so he could be independent.

2. The *goal* will help you reach your dreams. If not, you have the wrong goal. The goal gives you direction and a target to aim for. Chris's goal was IRONMAN® Florida in November 2020.

3. The *milestones* tell you if you are on track to achieve your goal. They are mini goals that collectively get you to your big goal. Chris's primary milestones were completing an Olympic triathlon in January and an IRONMAN 70.3® race in May.

4. The *strategy* describes how you will execute. Chris's strategy was "Get 1 percent better every day."

5. The *plan* consists of what you do every day to execute your strategy, hit your milestones, achieve your goal, and get your dreams. Chris wrote out his in ninety boxes that he checked off every day.

Chris's dream board takes up an entire wall, and people often ask me why that is. I want him to see it every morning, bigger than life, to remind him of what he needs to do. And I want him to write on it every night so he can celebrate what he did that day to get closer to achieving his dreams. I want him to read his dreams every day until they seep into his sub-conscious mind and become his new reality.

Let's take a closer look at the five components of the dream board:

1. The Dream

When Chris began his IRONMAN journey, I knew that he would need something powerful to motivate him on the long road ahead. Chris wanted to achieve something great, so it made sense that if God gave Chris the vision to be great, God would also give him a dream big enough to achieve it.

Here again is what Chris listed when I asked him to write down his dreams on the board:

1. Buy my own car
2. Buy my own house
3. Get a smoky-hot blond wife from Minnesota
4. Have my own money to take care of my family
5. Be a famous public speaker
6. Be a successful businessman

2. The Goal

Chris's dreams were supported by his goal of completing an IRONMAN competition. People often ask me questions like, Why an IRONMAN race? or Why such a big goal? My answer is simple: big dreams need big goals. When I told Chris he'd never realize his dreams sitting on the couch play-ing video games and watching TV, I also gave him a goal: If you do an IRONMAN triathlon and become a famous public speaker, you will have a chance to get your dreams. That became the anchor Chris needed to take him all the way to an IRONMAN race as well as put him on track toward the rest of his dreams.

When people ask me to comment on their goals, I often respond by asking them a couple of questions. First, What is the most important goal you have this year? And second, If you achieve that goal, will you be closer to realizing your dreams?

If the goal supports your dream, you have a great goal for yourself. That's it. That is the secret to goal setting. It's really simple, but people tend to overcomplicate goal setting. One goal is better than two, which is better than three, and so on. One goal keeps you focused, improves execution, and gives you a competitive advantage over people who split their time between multiple goals.

3. The Milestones

Whereas goals give you a target, milestones keep you headed in the right direction. Think of them as mini goals that keep you moving bit by bit toward your ultimate goal. Milestones help you keep track of how far you've come and how much further you have to go. They also help you get to your destination on time. Milestones should have weekly, monthly, and quarterly components to them.

Here are some milestones we used for Chris:

- **WEEKLY MILESTONES.** Every weekend Chris would do his long swim, bike, and run. Every week the milestone was for each event to be just a little farther or faster than the week before.

- **MONTHLY MILESTONES.** Every month we would try to do some kind of race and track results to see if Chris's overall pace was improving at a rate that told us we were on target.
- **QUARTERLY MILESTONES.** Every quarter we would see if Chris was progressing enough in speed or distance for a triathlon, going from a sprint in September to an Olympic in January to an IRONMAN 70.3 in May.

4. The Strategy

Strategy (the holy grail of our program and system) describes how you will execute. Chris had one purpose every day: to get 1 percent better. To make things simple for him, we used the concept of "one more" to reinforce the 1% Better strategy.

The idea was clear-cut: start with one of something and progress to your final goal. So when we were told that core strength was critical to all the other events, I picked a simple exercise for Chris to do: one push-up, one sit-up, and one squat. Then I taught Chris that 1 percent better means just one more. So two days later Chris did two sets of one of the exercises. Then three and four sets of another.

A year later, by the time Chris competed in IRONMAN Florida, he was doing four sets of 50 (or 200) push-ups, sit-ups, and squats. In May 2021, he was up to 360, and by the IRONMAN World Championship in Hawaii, Chris will be up to 500. That is the power of 1% Better. We also applied this principle to every other part of his training program.

The key is that Chris's journey to being an IRONMAN athlete did not follow a traditional training program. His approach was not about building his body using the optimal training strategy, but about building his mind to keep going and never quit until he did "one more." We knew that once we got his workouts to that point, when things got hard mentally in the IRONMAN event, he would not quit—and he did not.

Our conversations would go like this:

"Hey, buddy, today is your 1% Better core. How many did you do last time?"

He would look at his dream board and say, "I did four rounds of twenty-seven."

"Great," I would reply. "How many are we doing today?"

"I am doing four rounds of twenty-eight," he would answer.

That's it. He had developed a 1% Better mindset habit, and now it was easier to keep going and building on each day. The same conversation happened around his run, bike, and swim.

Keep in mind, this is a nontraditional system. A traditional workout system that you would get from a professional coach would be something like a 200-yard warm-up, then five 200s at 60 to 70 percent intensity with thirty seconds of rest, followed by five 100s at 80 percent intensity with sixty seconds of rest, and so on. Chris wouldn't have lasted a day with this approach, much less a week or longer. The traditional program is complex and very sophisticated. And I am sure it's very effective for the top 1 percent, those who have the ability, intelligence, and drive to succeed.

However, the 1% Better strategy is for the other 99 percent, those who are looking to succeed following a simple, although admittedly *slower*, path to a lifelong habit of continuous improvement and success. In the end, Chris still went from a 16-mile sprint marathon to a 140-mile IRONMAN triathlon in eleven months.

5. The Plan

The daily plan involves interacting with the dream board by filling in the ninety boxes with what you do every day to execute your strategy, hit your milestones, achieve your goal, and attain your dreams. There is power in the daily habit of writing down your activities and achievements and seeing them in the context of the rest of the dream board. It gets permanently embedded into your subconscious mind. It also helps you gain momentum because as you fill in more boxes, there will be fewer empty boxes, and you will see yourself getting closer and closer to your key milestones and your goal. I watched Chris get stronger mentally as he got closer to the end of each dream board.

Principle #2: The Metrics

The second principle for implementing the 1% Better plan is to measure the key performance indicators, or KPIs. Recording daily, weekly, monthly, and quarterly metrics is essential. As I discussed in chapter 10, always being able to see the correlation between the three groups of KPIs—leading, leaning, and lagging—and how each one affects the others is important. Without the right KPIs, the entire system falls apart. I understood the importance of KPIs but not specifically as they related to doing an IRONMAN triathlon. So I hired an expert, Hector Torres. He was an accomplished IRONMAN coach who had a system for measuring. While we did not agree on the training approach, we did agree on KPIs, and I appreciated his expertise and insights. Hector helped me set the right KPIs and targets, and he recommended a training plan for Chris, which I then modified to the 1% Better approach. I followed his plan in principle but not in the exact execution of it.

Since this is an area that needs much more attention than is the purpose of the book, I will just summarize the KPIs for IRONMAN event training as they related to Chris in each of these three groups:

Lead (Activities)	Lean (Achievements)	Lag (Results)
Strength and Bike: Days 1, 3 & 5 Swim and Run: Days 2, 4 & 6	One more each workout Weekly unit gains Weekly performance gains	Average speed per race 16-mile sprints 32-mile Olympic IRONMAN 70.3 IRONMAN triathlon

Principle #3: The Coaching Cadence

The third principle was a weekly cadence call between Chris's immediate team—including his guide, Dan; his training partner, Simone; and his triathlon coach, Hector—and me. These coaching calls had a consistent cadence, and we would focus on discussing the answers to these questions (I call it M4Q for "my four questions"):

1. What did Chris do over the last seven days?
2. What did Chris achieve these last seven days?
3. What did we learn during the last seven days?
4. What is Chris's activity and achievement plan for the next seven days?

This conversation was always anchored to the KPIs defined in Principle #2. This coaching call was sometimes contentious but always productive, and it created a culture of accountability, which led to continuous improvement. Our hearts and intentions were always good, but there were tense moments because people on the team were very successful people with type A personalities anchored in a traditional system, and here I was trying to design and implement a new system. The tension was caused by two key factors.

First, Chris is just different, and approaches that work for elite athletes do not work for him, so I had to relate everything they said to Chris, and they didn't always understand my translation.

Second, I understood the 1% Better system because I had been thinking about it and building it in the corporate world for years. I tried to explain it, but when people have spent their lives being successful in one system, they have little motivation to consider a different approach. All in all, it was an amazing experience, and we are blessed by an amazing team.

The coaching cadence principle is critical. So to increase your odds of success, you need a partner. This team represented our partners. I call this 1% Better together. Thus, the first thing you need to do when you start this program is find a partner who will do it with you.

HOW DO I START?

Now that you understand the 1% Better system, how should you start? My recommendation is to apply it specifically to exercise in your life. Why? Three reasons:

1. **IT'S EASY.** It is easy to start, do, and measure progress. It literally will cost you nothing and will be your foundation for everything. You can start by walking for cardio and doing push-ups, sit-ups, and squats for your core strength, and a year from now you will be a physical and mental giant.

2. **IT'S FOUNDATIONAL.** It will give you the physical strength and energy to perform better in every other area of your life. It is also scientifically proven that exercise increases the brain's capacity to learn, so through exercise you are increasing your brain power.

3. **IT CREATES A HABIT.** Most important, you are building the 1% Better mindset habit, which can then be applied to every other area of your life.

In chapter 13 I shared some simple lines I had created on a graph, an approach to achieving success that worked for Chris, so I know it can work for you too. Remember, however, to start and progress slowly because if you move too fast, you will hit a wall before you have the chance to develop the 1% Better mindset habit.

You need about nine months of steady progress to build it. Unlike most habits that are physical behaviors, this is a mental achievement habit. That is why I keep referring to it as the 1% Better mindset. If you do try to progress too quickly, your body will stop improving before you have had time to build a mental habit. Remember, the 1% Better plan is first about building the mind and then about building the body. The body will catch up eventually, but you must first build the mind.

You may see dramatic improvements early on, but if you start out too quickly, your progress is likely to flatline, and you'll be unable to stick with your plan for the duration. This flatlining effect is precisely what happens to most of us who pursue an improvement plan that emphasizes the big breakthroughs at the expense of smaller improvements.

The 1% Better plan is designed to provide long-term success and to do it as painlessly as possible. Think about it this way: most plans focus on getting you to the final result as quickly as possible. The 1% Better plan focuses on building your mind through a process. It is less concerned with a final result because your improvement never ends.

My prayer for you is that Chris's story inspires you to take action so you can be the person God meant you to be. Your next step is to accept Chris's challenge to get 1% Better for thirty days and to help a person with special needs do the same.

Go to ChrisNikic.com for additional information on how to start building your own plan.

NOTES

1. "World Population by Year," Worldometer, accessed April 11, 2021, https://www.worldometers.info/world-population/world-population-by-year/.
2. Russell Cox, "A Look at Ironman Participation Statistics," CoachCox, August 27, 2018, https://www.coachcox.co.uk/2018/08/27/a-look-at-ironman-participation-statistics/.
3. "The IRONMAN Story," History, IRONMAN Group, accessed April 11, 2021, https://www.ironman.com/history.
4. "The IRONMAN Story."
5. "The IRONMAN Story."
6. Special Olympics, "Special Olympics Announces New Global and Inaugural Champion Ambassador Programs," Cision PR Newswire, December 3, 2020, https://www.prnewswire.com/news-releases/special-olympics-announces-new-global-and-inaugural-champion-ambassador-programs-301185781.html.
7. "Sir Roger Bannister," Academy of Achievement, last revised February 19, 2021, https://achievement.org/achiever/sir-roger-bannister-2/.

8. Roger Bannister, *The Four-Minute Mile*, rev. 50th anniversary ed. (2004; repr. Guilford, CT: Lyons Press, 2018), 201.

9. Stephen Guise, *Mini Habits: Smaller Habits, Bigger Results* (Seattle: Selective Entertainment, 2013).

10. Phillippa Lally, Cornelia H. M. van Jaarsveld, Henry W. W. Potts, and Jane Wardle, "How Are Habits Formed: Modelling Habit Formation in the Real World," *European Journal of Social Psychology* 40, no. 6 (July 16, 2009): https://doi.org/10.1002/ejsp.674.

11. Phillippa Lally, "How Are Habits Formed."

12. Stephen Guise, *Mini Habits: Smaller Habits, Bigger Results* (Seattle: Selective Entertainment, 2013).

ABOUT THE AUTHORS

CHRIS NIKIC is the twenty-one-year-old man who made history as the first person with Down syndrome to complete a full distance IRONMAN® triathlon. Guinness World Records recognized Chris's achievement after he finished a 2.4-mile swim, a 112-mile bike ride, and a 26.2-mile run at the 2020 Visit Panama City Beach IRONMAN Florida. He completed the race in 16 hours, 46 minutes, and 9 seconds—14 minutes under the 17-hour cutoff time.

Chris and his father, Nik, developed the 1% Better Challenge to help Chris stay motivated during training. What drives Chris is this: "My mission is to honor God by being the best me I can be so I can be an example to others. I want to change the perceptions and raise expectations for others like me so we can reach our God-given potential. Believe and achieve by getting 1 percent better."

Chris is a 2021 EPSY winner, receiving the Jimmy V Award for Perseverance. He also continued his training for the 2021 IRONMAN World Championship in Kona, Hawaii, as well as the 2022 Special Olympics USA Games, and is a Champion Ambassador for Special Olympics.

chrisnikic.com/books

NIK NIKIC has more than twenty years of experience in helping clients maximize top-line revenue. Nik's expertise is focused on developing a sales performance optimization system through a hybrid approach of integrating sales process, customer relationship management tools, and sales skills into one cohesive solution.

Over the years Nik and his organization have worked with many global companies, such as United Technologies, Toshiba, Deloitte, Ricoh, Tech Data, Progress Energy, Clear Channel, Siemens, Xerox, The Gartner Group, EMC Corporation, Parametric Technology, SCT, Cambridge Technology, GE Capital, Oce/Imagistics, NICE Systems, and many others.

Nik is the father of Chris Nikic, the first person with Down syndrome ever to complete a full distance IRONMAN® triathlon. Together they developed the 1% Better Challenge to help Chris stay motivated during his training. Having trained thousands of people during his career, Nik says, "Chris is the most coachable person I've ever met."

DON YAEGER is an eleven-time *New York Times* bestselling author, longtime associate editor at *Sports Illustrated*, and one of the most in-demand public speakers on the corporate circuit today. He delivers about seventy speeches a year to an average annual audience of nearly a hundred thousand. He also hosts the popular *Corporate Competitor Podcast*. He lives in Tallahassee, Florida, with his wife and two children, ages eleven and twelve.